THE GIFT OF GIVING

WAYNE WATTS

NAVPRESS
A MINISTRY OF THE NAVIGATORS
P.O. Box 6000, Colorado Springs, CO 80934

© 1982 by the Watts Foundation
All rights reserved, including translation
ISBN: 0-89109-491-1
14910

Co-published with the International Evangelism Association, 3850 South Freeway (Post Office Box 6883), Fort Worth, Texas 76115

To my precious wife

FRANCES

*who first
taught me about
tithing and giving.*

*Her deep and abiding faith
in our Savior and His word has
permeated our entire family. She
is truly God's gift to me.*

CONTENTS

FOREWORD

Wayne Watts is a dear friend, a Christian brother, and a man's man. In the years I have known him (nearly twenty-five now) I've concluded that he will not say no to Christ at any point. He practices what he preaches.

This book is the most thoroughly biblical handling of the subject of giving I have seen. Yet it is eminently practical in its application. Wayne is an intense Bible scholar and inspirational Bible expositor, and he has a lifestyle which makes him readily recognized as a practicing follower of Christ. You may not like his conclusions, and they may not fit your grid—or prejudices—but you will find it difficult to fault his interpretation of the Holy Scriptures.

He has been deeply involved with his local church, International Evangelism Association, Bible Memory Association, the World Discipleship Development Foundation, and The Navigators, to mention just a few. He has been successful as a petroleum engineer, entrepreneur, and trader in the oil business.

The longer I've known Wayne the more I've grown to appreciate him. I'm grateful that now you will have the joy, as the curtains of his life are parted just a little, to look in. May what you see cause you to love Jesus Christ more deeply and to appreciate anew how He can and will manifest Himself through a life of giving.

Gene Warr

ACKNOWLEDGMENTS

My sincere thanks to all those who have prayed for this book, especially my family, Tom and Waynette Welch, Bill and Mary Ann Watts, Don and Linda Bradley, and Bob and Sharon Zamorano.

I would also like to thank my faithful daily prayer partners who have for more than twenty years constantly prayed for me: Charles Featherston, Jack Humphreys, Bob Potter, Charlie Riggs, Donald Tabb, Gene Warr, and Harold Warren.

Words of special appreciation go to the following people who gave input on this book from start to finish:

Billie Hanks, Jr., and Gene Warr, who prayed continuously, encouraged me, critiqued the work at intervals, and called to push me gently to *"get on with it."*

Linda Watts Bradley, who encouraged me and helped me rearrange the material.

Bill and Marge Shell, who made helpful suggestions along the way and encouraged me.

Deonne Beshear and Reba Whitehurst, who were faithful to type, arrange, and rearrange the manuscript.

Lauren Libby and Betty Skinner, whose encouraging phone calls and letters at strategic times supported me in this work.

Keith Marion and Ken Williams, who helped me many times along the way.

Chapter ONE

HOW THIS BOOK CAME TO BE

When I was ten years old I had an experience which convinced me God had a purpose in my life. A buddy and I were out checking our traps for game on a winter day in a bitterly cold north Texas gale. About the time we finished checking the traps rain began to fall, and in order to get out of the cold and rain we crouched in a small ravine under an overhanging limestone rock.

The space we were crouching in went back about four feet into the side of the hill. The ledge we were under was about a foot thick, four feet wide, fifteen feet long, and must have weighed tons. To keep warm we built a big fire, but before long there was so much heat in this limited space under the rock that we were forced outside to cool off. Just as we stepped out from under our limestone shelter, the entire slab crashed down on the fire and the place where we had been crouching only a few seconds before.

I still remember the conviction that settled over me then that God had spared my life. He had moved me from certain death to give me an opportunity to live and to fulfill the purpose for which I was created. The unfolding of events in my life since that day has gradually strengthened my conviction. I didn't know then what that purpose would be or all the ways He would lead me to find Christ as my Savior and Lord and to serve Him.

After I became a Christian and began to study the Bible, I became intensely interested in what God says the Christian's attitude toward material resources should be. I found that God is vitally concerned about how we use the money he has entrusted to us, and particularly how we give.

I suppose my interest in money stemmed from my earliest childhood. As far back as I can remember it seemed to me that the whole world revolved around money. My father had died when I was six years old, leaving us with no money. I remember how almost daily I would go to my mother and ask for a nickel (that was all you needed in those days) to buy something. As I became older, everything I wanted to do was based on "Do I have enough money?" or "Can I get enough money to do that?"

After I graduated from the University of Texas, I

went to work to make enough money to do the things that were supposed to make a person happy. With a degree in petroleum engineering, I got a job as engineer for an independent oil producer in west central Texas. Our philosophy in business was to search out "stripper" leases (leases that had the flush oil already taken out and in which the flow of oil had diminished so that pumping was required). Our goal was to determine if we could buy a 15-barrel lease with a few wells and by certain techniques end up with a 25-barrel lease. By so doing, we could get our purchase price back in three years rather than five or six years; thus the profits would start sooner.

Almost from the beginning we were successful, and at first this success brought great satisfaction to my heart. Even though I did not at this time own an interest in any of these properties, I got much of the credit for their success, and my pride ran high. I worked harder than ever to get more praise and, as a result, more salary.

But after a few years of this I began to be frustrated. The new deals did not produce the old happiness any more. The approval and applause of the oil men sounded hollow. I had times of deep depression. Fear gripped me and darkness would frequently come over my mind. I found the only answer to depression was keeping busy, so I put in long hours of hard labor.

This kind of activity worked well until I would get a virus of some sort and could not go to work. During these times of inactivity when I was confined to staying

13

around home, I would think about dying—and then I would really get sick. This fear continued periodically until I was more than thirty years old. All along the way our company was growing, but the fear of death plagued me. I was frustrated with trying to silence that persistent voice which reminded me that death was coming, perhaps sooner than later.

I tried to gain peace through making a financial deal with God. My wife, who had become a Christian at age twelve, was a firm believer in "tithing" or giving a tenth of one's income to God, and she tried early to get me to tithe. My answer had always been, "How can we tithe when we are spending more money than we are making?" Her standard answer was, "I don't know how, but it works." She must have learned that in Sunday school.

Despite my unbelieving approach to everything, including finances, she persisted. Finally at the height of my frustration I made a deal with God. I said something like this: "Lord, if you will give me inward peace, I will double my giving each year." Now that is a dumb kind of a deal to make, and of course I couldn't carry out my promise. You try doubling your giving from $200 per year each year for the next five years. It goes like this: $200, $400, $800, $1,600, $3,200. That last figure was half of my salary in the late 1930s and early 40s. The next year would have taken all my salary.

God later gave me peace when I accepted Christ as my Savior, but that peace was *on His terms*: "Without money, and without price" (Isaiah 55:1). Through faith alone I invited Him to come into my heart and take over my life. He did come in, and I became a new creature in Christ—redeemed not with silver or gold, but by the precious blood of Jesus Christ shed on Calvary's cross for my sins. After that experience my depression and fear of death ceased and never returned.

After I was born again my perspective on many things, including money, began gradually to change. One of the hardest lessons I had to learn was to let God control my financial decisions. I found that when He directed my choices, even missed opportunities became blessings, both spiritually and financially.

I vividly recall one incident that helped me learn to trust God to guide me in financial decisions. My partner and I had been in business a good many years working mainly on small deals. Then a rather large oil company wanted to sell, and it looked like we had the opportunity to buy them out completely. (You need to know that I owned a very small interest in our partnership. Also, on larger deals we would share the investment with a good friend, so my interests were even smaller then.)

For nearly a year we studied the larger company's changing valuation as they continued to drill new wells. Finally the time came for us to make a decision, and we prepared to make a serious effort to bring the deal to a close. I would normally have done the trading, but this time Mr. Fleming, who was going to finance the deal and carry an interest, wanted to do the negotiating.

On the morning of the day we had set to meet the owner and make our offer, Mr. Fleming spent two hours with my partner and me going over the summary sheets and values. We had prayed much about this deal. We agreed together that we could go as high as two million dollars, but we would start at $1.8 million.

We left our office and walked the two blocks to the appointed meeting place. I felt sure I knew how things should go. After about thirty minutes of small talk, Mr. Fleming made the owner an offer of $1.8 million. This offer disappointed the owner and we spent another fifteen minutes doing what negotiators call "hard trading." I kept waiting for Mr. Fleming to go up to $1.9 million, which I felt the owner might accept. I was sure he would accept two million. But Mr. Fleming never moved from his original offer and the deal did not close. I could hardly believe what had happened. I dared not question Mr. Fleming's judgment in business decisions —especially this one, since he was financing the project.

For the rest of that day and night I was sick at heart, frustrated, depressed, and hard to live with. Finally the truth hit me that God really was in control of all things. As soon as I accepted the reality of God's sovereignty, joy began to take over, and I slept peacefully.

A few months later the best deal of my life came along. It was over twice the size of the one we had lost, and it eventually grew to three times as much value. Within two months we had this new deal evaluated, financed, and purchased.

If we had bought the first property, we would not have been able to finance the second deal five months later. God definitely intervened in that negotiating session on the first deal so we would be in a position to purchase the larger and better property five months later. God is faithful and always has our best interest at heart when we recognize His ownership and His desires for us as revealed in the Bible: "In everything give thanks, for this is the will of God in Christ Jesus concerning you" (1 Thessalonians 5:18).

Another step along the way of my spiritual growth was when I learned that as you make more money, you get added joy by giving it to worthwhile causes. That conviction came to me over a period of several years. God led me, not without many struggles and defeats, to step out in faith and begin to claim His promises.

Following my conversion, my interest in giving was spurred by my church's annual fundraising activities. I noticed that at a certain time each year there was a great emphasis on raising the church budget by having everyone sign pledges so we could operate another year. During these concentrated "drives," many choice Bible verses were quoted about what God could and would provide for His own. But during the other eleven months of the year, very little was said about giving.

Later I had the privilege of serving on the board of my church and the boards of several wonderful Christian organizations. I noticed they were always short of money. Much good work needed to be done, but too

17

often the necessary funds were lacking. Their theme song seemed to be "We don't have enough money!"

In each instance I asked the leader two questions: "What do you teach your people about biblical principles of giving?" and "How consistently are these truths being shared?" Through such questions I learned that (1) comparatively little is being taught, and (2) the teaching comes only once a year during the budget drive.

My interest grew year after year, until I questioned the leaders of three large tax-exempt organizations regarding this problem. Each of them needed more money to pursue the job God had called him to do. But not one of them offered a complete Bible study on scriptural giving. My frank response to these organizations was, "You are reaping exactly what you are sowing."

As I thought about this problem, the Lord began to show me practical answers. I discovered that God's word is full of specific instructions regarding our giving. He finally got my full attention when I saw how so much evil is related in one way or another to the love of money: "The love of money is a root of *all kinds of evil*" (1 Timothy 6:10, NIV).

As my concern developed over many years, the Lord laid it on my heart to gather together from the Bible His basic teachings regarding money. This book is the result of that study. I found that Scripture gives us a complete blueprint for giving. It contains all the promises needed to enable us to do *His work His way*. The theme song of every Christian church and organization can and should be, "The lack of money is *not* our basic problem." The same is true for the individual Christian. The answer to our problem in giving is to learn to practice what the Bible teaches rather than to continue living a nonvictorious life. God has the only perfect plan.

This book has been written for three purposes: (1) to encourage those who have never received Christ as Savior to do so; (2) to challenge Christians who have never made Christ the Lord of their lives to make that decision; and (3) to instruct fellow believers who have never understood clearly God's way of giving, that they may put into practice and enjoy the benefits of living according to these biblical principles.

Chapter TWO

GOD OWNS EVERYTHING

To develop our perspective on giving, let us first see what the Bible says about ownership. God's ownership of the world is clearly stated in <u>Psalm 24:1—"The earth is the Lord's and the fullness thereof, the world and they that dwell therein</u>." The principle of His ownership is based on the truth that in the beginning God came from nowhere, because there was nowhere to come from. When He created the world and all that is in it, He stood on nothing because there was nothing to stand on. He created everything out of nothing, because there was nothing around to use. *He is God!* He certainly owns everything, and He made enough of everything for our use.

I discovered the real meaning of God's divine ownership of everything as I was doing a detailed study of the life of Abraham. Genesis 13 tells how Abraham and Lot were forced to divide the common grazing land because their respective herdsmen were beginning to fight over the grazing rights. Even though God had promised all the land to him, Abraham first let Lot choose the portion of land that he would take. Lot, true to his nature, chose the best grazing land—the "well-watered plain"—and Abraham took the less valuable land that was left.

On the surface it looked as if Abraham had suffered a tremendous financial loss. But Abraham knew that neither he nor Lot owned the land—God did—so in reality the property was not changing ownership. The only difference now, after the division, was that each of them would have stewardship responsibilities on different land—land that God actually owned.

At the same time I was studying Abraham's dealing with Lot, I was engaged in selling all of my properties to my partner. God's leadership through the example of Abraham caused me to let my partner set the price. The next year the price of oil increased from three dollars per barrel to more than thirty. Even though my friends tried to offer me sympathy for what they considered to be a terrible mistake, I had deep peace about it because I knew God directed me. My experiences in subsequent years have shown me without question that obedience to God is never a mistake.

However, we often fail to use God's resources for God's glory. So we should ask ourselves this question: <u>Am I making decisions and living as if things belong to God or to me?</u> The way we live unmistakably declares the answer.

God has never relinquished His title deed to the world, and He never will. The Bible teaches that we are to be faithful "stewards" of all that God has made. He has given us basic principles to help us be faithful in this stewardship.

One example is the parable Jesus gave us in Luke 19:12-27. His opening words were, "A nobleman living in a certain province was called away to the distant capital of the empire to be crowned king of his province. Before he left he called together ten assistants and gave them each $2,000 to invest while he was gone" (19:12-13, *Living Bible*). Their assigned work was to be productive in business.

Jesus went on to say that upon the nobleman's return he called the ten servants to account, asking what they had done with the money. Those who had invested wisely received a reward. But one servant, because he was fearful, simply buried the money, then dug it up and gave it back because he knew the nobleman was hard to please and he was afraid he would lose the money. The nobleman reprimanded this servant: "You vile and wicked slave. Hard, am I? That's exactly how I'll be toward you! If you knew so much about me and how tough I am, then why didn't you deposit the money in the bank so I

23

could at least get some interest on it?" (19:22-23, *Living Bible*). We must never forget that God is the rightful owner of everything, and *we are all personally accountable for what we do with His money*.

For example, today many people are transferring assets to their children to avoid inheritance taxes. These parents have considered the business of making money a top priority in their lives. In many situations their children have a perfect record of consistently *losing money* in every business investment they make. Even with this record, little by little, the parents continue transferring all their assets into the legal control of their children. Why? Because they do not really know what God teaches in the Bible about *ownership*. Giving God's money to children who lack wisdom is being a poor steward of God's resources. What we should do is *teach our children the truth about money as revealed in the Scriptures*, and then ask the Holy Spirit to lead them in how, when, and where to do their own giving and investing.

Let me suggest a practical way to explain to your children the reasons you contribute to certain ministries. Plan a trip with them to visit these organizations. Together, find out answers to questions like these: Is your organization fulfilling the Great Commission? Are your staff members practicing believers? Do the staff love one another? Is your overall operation efficient?

If you are checking a school or seminary, get the address of graduates who live in your area and interview them. Learn their basic vision and perspective: the way they set up their priorities; what they believe about Jesus Christ and the Bible; how much they are involved in prayer, devotions, Bible study, and evangelism; and how much unity in the Spirit is evident in their relationships in the home.

If the graduates from the Christian schools you support think and live the same way that non-Christian men and women do, you may want to encourage leaders in these schools to correct their course so they get on their heart what is on Jesus' heart. Or, you may decide to change your gifts to other Christian works.

In general, there should be a tremendous difference in life objectives between graduates of secular schools and Christian schools (though I realize that many good Christian young people go to secular universities, and because of their solid devotional life and warm fellowship and service in a Christian group, they not only survive the humanistic atmosphere but also effectively minister to the pagans on their campuses. Also, many professors in secular schools use their position as a platform to help students find a meaningful life in Christ.) Find out if graduates of the Christian schools you support are really disciples of Christ. For it is God's money you are spending.

I vividly remember a man who had large assets in oil and who discovered a new oil field and doubled his income. A few days later a good friend of his asked, "How does it feel to have your income double overnight?" He thought a moment and then replied, "My assets have not changed—I did not own the first money, so I own the same amount now as before, which is zero. I feel added responsibility to God for managing this new asset."

In reality we all own the same amount of money— zero! However, each of us will be held accountable for the money entrusted to us to use for God's glory—"Unto whomsoever much is given, shall be much required" (Luke 12:48).

A good friend once told a story about his father, who knew little or nothing about God's ownership. The man was a wealthy drilling contractor and gave large gifts. The entire city knew about these gifts. But eventually he began to lose money in his business and went broke. Yet through his trials he apparently learned a biblical principle, because when people asked him, "Would you like to have some of those gifts back, now that you are broke?" his answer was always the same: "No, if I had not given that money away, I would have lost it too."

Why do you give money? Here is a good question to test your motives. Would you give what you give if *no one ever knew*—not your wife or husband, friends, bankers, or the government—no one but God? That's a good question to ask ourselves to find out *why we really give*. All too often, we love "the praise from men more than praise from God" (John 12:43).

That which we have given in the support of God's work becomes in a unique way really ours, and cannot be taken away when we come to the end of the road. The only thing we can take with us in our dead, cold hands is that which we have *given away*. Jesus said, "Lay not up for yourselves treasures upon earth, where moth and rust doth corrupt, and where thieves break through and steal. But lay up for yourselves treasures in heaven, where neither moth nor rust doth corrupt, and where thieves do not break through nor steal; for where your treasure is, there will your heart be also" (Matthew 6:19-21).

Note well: If a man's treasures are in heaven, *he* will be planning to go there too!

Chapter THREE

DOES TEN PERCENT OF OUR INCOME BELONG TO GOD?

Perhaps you are wondering why giving ten percent of one's income has been a common practice among Christians for centuries. A gift of ten percent, called a "tithe" in the Bible, first appeared in the time of Abraham, more than four hundred years before God gave the Ten Commandments to Moses. In these early Bible times God must have given Abraham instructions to tithe.

We find in the fourteenth chapter of Genesis that after his battle with the kings, Abraham gave a tenth of the spoils of his victory to God's priest, Melchizedek. Giving his tithe was an act of worship. In view of the covenants and promises that God made to Abraham it was also an expression of his conviction that God owned everything he had.

Abraham's grandson, Jacob, followed Abraham's example by giving a tithe. When Jacob was fleeing from his brother's wrath, he was shown a vision of a beautiful stairway to heaven (Genesis 28:10-22). At the end of this encounter with God, Jacob said, "Of all that Thou shalt give me, I will surely give the tenth unto Thee" (verse 22). This passage underscores the fact that Jacob knew everything belonged to God. As the Scripture says, "The earth is the Lord's and the fullness thereof" (Psalm 24:1).

Later, in the law given to Moses, God told Israel that ten percent of all a man possessed should be set aside for God. "And all the tithe of the land, whether of the seed of the land, or of the fruit of the tree, is the Lord's" (Leviticus 27:30).

Does this principle of the tithe apply to the Christian today? Yes. Although the main details of the tithe are contained in the Old Testament, Jesus put His stamp of approval on this practice in the New Testament (Matthew 23:23, Luke 11:42).

In fact, the principle of divine ownership, which the tithe represented, was expanded and deepened by Christ to include the whole man. Jesus laid down this principle as the condition for discipleship: "Whosoever there be among you that forsaketh not all that he has, he cannot be My disciple" (Luke 14:33). The Christian, a "new creature" living by the power of the Holy Spirit, is asked by Christ to surrender his money, talents, time, possessions, and even his very life.

Paul expressed it this way: "I beseech you, therefore, brethren by the mercies of God, that ye present your bodies a living sacrifice" (Romans 12:1). This New Testament appeal for living in total consecration intensifies the principle taught in the tithe.

Many Christians, however, have never experienced freedom from the tyranny of material things, a freedom that total consecration brings. But to those disciples who are sincerely trying to follow Christ, giving money to God is of vital importance because it is a tangible acknowledgment of the fact that He owns everything they have.

When a committed Christian asks how and where to begin giving, the historic scriptural practice of the tithe is helpful. It is a *guide to minimum giving*.

GIVING THE FIRST INCOME

Using agricultural terms, the Bible speaks of the tithe as coming out of the "first fruits" of a crop. In terms of money, this means the first ten percent of our income. Before any of our income is used for personal needs, God's tithe should first be given. Many of us have waited until the end of the month or year to give our tithe, only to find that it was already spent. Too late we discover it has been spent for personal desires related to family or business. To avoid temptation, we must be careful to set aside and give the *first* portion of our paycheck or in-

31

come, leaving the other ninety percent to use as God directs for household expenses, business purposes, or additional giving. He is Lord of *all* we have.

I know a man who is deeply committed to Christ and who looks forward with enthusiasm to giving his tithe consistently. Because his particular kind of income is spread through the month, he puts ten percent of each check he receives into a *tithe account*. By the end of each month, he clears out the account. In this way, he overcomes the temptation to misuse God's tithe for personal or investment purposes. When this man dies, he will not have to slink around, fearing to face God because of what he knows is left unused in God's account.

Satan will try to say, "Don't give your tithe now. Wait until you get enough to do a really big project for God." Such reasoning is diametrically opposed to God's plan! He says, "out of the *first* fruits!" This kind of continual "first fruits" giving is designed to bring us joy repeatedly as we give to God *first* out of our income.

The Scripture says, "Honor the Lord by giving Him the first part of all your income, and He will fill your barns" (Proverbs 3:9-10, *Living Bible*). I have observed that if we obey God in faith, He will enable us to accomplish far more with the ninety percent that is left than we could have done with the original one hundred percent.

"First-fruits" giving has always been God's special way of teaching His people to be like Him. He is a giver, and He wants to lead His children to be conformed to His likeness. Giving is an important part of the process of developing Christian character. *As we give, we grow spiritually*—learning to honor and reverence God and to always put Him first. Although Spirit-led giving has a vital part in helping the church and Christian organizations carry out their mission, we must remember that its *primary* purpose is not to help God pay His bills, but to help us grow more like Christ.

It is obvious from the following Scriptures that God wants to have fellowship with His children through their giving: "You must tithe all of your crops every year. Bring this tithe to eat before the Lord your God at the place He shall choose as His sanctuary; this applies to your tithes of grain, new wine, olive oil, and the firstborn of your flocks and herds. The purpose of tithing is to teach you always to put God first in your lives" (Deuteronomy 14:22-23, *Living Bible*). To have fellowship with Him we must put Him first and reverence Him. Giving will start us on the road to being more and more like Him—a giving and loving person.

David expressed it this way: "But who am I and who are my people that we should be permitted to give anything to You? Everything we have has come from You, and we only give You what is Yours already (1 Chronicles 29:14, *Living Bible*).

Giving is a vital part of living abundantly by faith. Deuteronomy 11:24-25 further emphasizes this point: "It is possible to give away and become richer! It is also

33

possible to hold on too tightly and lose everything. Yes, the liberal man shall be rich! By watering others, he waters himself" (*Living Bible*).

STEALING FROM GOD?

In the days of the prophet Malachi, God said: "Will a man rob God? Surely not! And yet you have robbed Me. . . . You have robbed Me of the tithes and offerings due to Me" (Malachi 3:8, *Living Bible*). Today, as in that day, God has first claim on our resources. If we do not obey His word and give, are not we also stealing from God? Obedience is the key to blessing. When we obey His will He gives us additional blessings. If we refuse to give as He directs, we hinder Him from pouring out His blessing upon us. Our greed is our own worst enemy, because by grasping what we have we are unable to receive more.

When an oil man leases land from a property owner, the normal override or royalty kept by the owner is one-eighth—12.5 percent. The oil operator is never allowed to keep any of the eighth which belongs to the property owner. If he did keep it, the property owner would bring legal action against him for stealing and would easily recover his *rightful* part of the money. In the same way we could say that by giving ten percent, we have only returned to God His override, or what was His in the first place. Our own *giving* starts beyond the ten percent.

Chapter FOUR

GIVING IS WORSHIP

While researching the biblical principles of giving, I considered the subject of worship. Frankly, I had never before studied worship in detail to find God's point of view. I have come to the conclusion that giving, along with our thanksgiving and praise, is worship.

In the past I made pledges to my church to be paid on a yearly basis. Once a month, I would write a check while in church and drop it in the collection plate. Sometimes I would mail a check from my office. My objective was for the church to get the total pledge before the end of the year. Though I had already experienced the joy of giving, the *act* of making my gift had little relationship to worship.

While I was writing this book God convicted me to begin giving every time I went to church. The verse that spoke to me about this was Deuteronomy 16:16—"Do not appear before Me empty-handed." When I started doing this, if a check were not handy, I gave cash. At first I thought about keeping up with the money given. Then God convicted me again. He seemed to say, "You do not need to keep up with the amount of cash. Give to Me simply out of a heart of love, and see how much you enjoy the service." I made this change in giving habits, and it has greatly enhanced my joy in our worship services.

WE WORSHIP WHAT WE LOVE

Many of us know by heart what Jesus called the greatest commandment: "Thou shalt love the Lord thy God with all thy heart. . . ." But we know little about expressing this love through giving. In the writings of Moses we are told that the Lord drew His people to Himself at a special place of worship. Though the distances were great and many had to walk, still they came to express their devotion to God. Continually He sought to build their faith and deepen their character by teaching them how to express their love.

For this reason, Scripture says, "Every man shall give as he is able, according to the blessing of the Lord thy God which He hath given thee" (Deuteronomy 16:17). This passage reveals two important principles: First, God is leading *everyone* to give. And second, we are to give as we have been blessed. This same principle

is taught by the apostle Paul in 1 Corinthians 16:2—
"Upon the first day of the week let every one of you lay by him in store, as God hath prospered him."

In Deuteronomy 16:10-11 we find an additional emphasis: "Then you shall celebrate . . . with a freewill offering of your hand, which you shall give just as the Lord your God blesses you, and you shall rejoice before the Lord your God." This gift was to be over and above the tithe which had already been reserved by God out of the "first fruits." Why this additional instruction on giving?

Man's heart is so constructed that he will worship what he *really* loves. We worship what we love—we love what we worship. Inevitably, a man will spend time and money on that which he loves deeply. In Deuteronomy 16:17 the expression *"give as he is able"* does not refer only to giving in proportion to one's earnings. As a matter of practice, most people *do* give in proportion to what they earn. But the words "as he is able" also relate to a man's spirituality. Ultimately we give as we are *enabled* by our spiritual growth and maturity. We have trouble giving when it is not done on the basis of faith and obedience. For example, if the Lord tells us to make a specific gift separate and apart from our tithe, we may react by saying, "Lord, I can't do that." This statement is exactly right. *We* can't do it—but He can: Our sufficiency is not of self but of God (2 Corinthians 3:5).

It is important that we give as God directs, and not simply impulsively or out of fleshly motives. I have a good friend of long standing who was both aggressive as a businessman and abounding in spiritual activities. He actually neglected his business to "serve the Lord." We were both part of a group of businessmen who worked as a team in Christian service. Every time this group wanted someone to go witnessing, to speak at meetings, or to join us in giving money to needy Christian causes, he was always in on the project on the same basis as the rest of us. The problem, as we found out later, was that he was giving out of his own resources—and he simply did not have enough resources. His excesses finally caught up with him when his business failed. He was so anxious to serve the Lord "like the others" and to always be in on the action, that he would "over-commit." He "over-served" out of enthusiasm before he had truly learned how to understand God's leading. He overextended himself in time as well as money.

This man finally removed himself from business and went full-time into the ministry. When his business books were closed he owed about forty thousand dollars. I am happy to report that at the end of seven years, God so convicted him of his unpaid debts that he went back into business and in five years paid off his entire debt. Today this man has a good balance between business and ministry. He is one of the most effective Christian businessmen I know.

Warning: Do not overcommit your time or money. God never gets in a hurry! In the gospels I never see Jesus running, but always see Him walking. God has perfect timing for all of us. I know from experience how easy it is to get priorities rearranged in order to satisfy my ego and become a "people-pleaser."

Spirit-led giving leads us into a new dimension of joy because we are amazed to see God use us far beyond our expectations. When Scripture says, "I can do all things through Him who strengthens me" (Philippians 4:13, NASB) this includes spiritual giving as well.

WHAT GIFTS PLEASE GOD?

God is not impressed by the *size* of our gifts, but He is pleased by what we give out of specific obedience. This demonstrates our love for Him. The widow's example speaks volumes about a gift that pleases God:

> And He sat down opposite the treasury, and began observing how the multitude were putting money into the treasury; and many rich people were putting in large sums. And a poor widow came and put in two small copper coins, which amount to a cent. And calling His disciples to Him, He said to them, "Truly I say to you, this poor widow put in more than all the contributors to the treasury; for they all put in out of their surplus, but she, out of her poverty, put in all she owned, all she had to live on." (Mark 12:41-44, NASB)

An analysis of this passage reveals several interesting insights:

1. When you give to the Lord, He watches you with interest, just as He did in the case of this widow.
2. When you give, your gift can be a positive exam-

ple to others. Jesus wanted His disciples to learn from the sacrificial gift of this godly woman.

3. A sacrificial gift means far more to God than gifts given out of surplus income, where the element of sacrifice and faith are not required.

Paul shed light on the motive in giving which pleases God when he wrote this to the early believers in Corinth: "If you are really eager to give, then it isn't important how much you have to give. God wants you to give what you have, not what you do not have" (2 Corinthians 8:12, *Living Bible*).

It is clear that either a very small or a very large gift can be totally pleasing to God. Our motivation for making the gift is what God looks at.

The following story is told about the wealthy industrialist and inventor, R. G. LeTourneau. When he was a boy, God led him to give a ten-dollar offering to missions. It so happened that ten dollars represented his total earnings, saved from doing various jobs. Years later when he told about this, a lady reportedly asked him this question: "Mr. LeTourneau, as a boy you trusted God enough to give Him everything. Would you be willing to do that again today?" LeTourneau answered her, "Without a doubt!" His life was a living example of his answer. It was his practice to give ninety percent of his income to the cause of Christian growth and world evangelization.

Once a friend told me of his surprise when he saw LeTourneau's home in east Texas. At this time in Le-

Tourneau's life, God had so blessed him financially that he could have afforded a palace, but he chose to live in a modest home similar to that of his neighbors. Both he and the widow in Jesus' day were motivated by the desire to put God first in their lives, and they expressed this desire through their maximum giving.

MAXIMUM GIVING

You may be asking, "What is maximum giving?" My reply is simple. The money we have is not from the government or our business, but from God. Therefore He alone can determine the maximum. "For it is He who is giving you power to make wealth" (Deuteronomy 8:18, NASB). *God is our source.*

I vividly remember an incident that happened while we were enlarging our church building. This addition was supposed to cost $500,000, but before it was finished, it cost $600,000. To raise the additional money, thirty men met together, among whom was a rather wealthy man. During the meeting he began to make excuses for the small pledge he originally had made. He also explained why he could not give more now. He basically said, "I have given all the money the Internal Revenue Service will *allow* me to give this year."

After the meeting, a good friend of his put his arm around the man's shoulders and whispered, "Tom, when are you going to stop giving the government's money away and start giving some of your own?" This

41

man's understanding of maximum giving was not determined through prayer or by God's leading. His concept was based on the maximum tax-deductible benefit which the government would allow in a year's business.

Actually, more than half of the contributions this man generally gave would have otherwise been paid as taxes anyway, so the amount he was actually parting with was only a fraction of the dollars given.

It seems to me, after looking closely at the account of the poor widow's gift of two copper coins, that God is extremely pleased by the spirit of love that causes people to give *above* the government allowance for deductions on taxes. If we are looking to the government as our source, then we must never give above what the government allows us to give. But if we are looking to God as our source, we need to forget the maximum allowable for deduction and give as the Holy Spirit guides and prompts us. *God is our source!*

So far as I know, the United States is the only country in the world where gifts to the church are deductible from one's income tax. Would your giving pattern change if this law were changed? If so, why?

Chapter FIVE

THE LOVE OF MONEY

Scripture warns us in 1 Timothy 6:9-10 about the dangers of a desire to get rich:

> People who want to get rich fall into temptation and a trap and into many foolish and harmful desires that plunge men into ruin and destruction. For the love of money is a root of all kinds of evil. Some people, eager for money, have wandered from the faith and pierced themselves with many griefs. (NIV)

Yet despite these clear warnings, the heart of man naturally desires wealth, even though it harms his faith and hurts him physically and mentally.

A most revealing message about this is tucked away

43

in the book of Judges. This book is a record of failures, because during that period of time "every man did that which was right in his own eyes" (Judges 17:6). Many of God's people had fallen into paganism and idolatry and were no longer attempting to worship the true and living God.

In Judges 17:1-4 we read about a woman who had apparently been saving money to give to God. Then one day the money was missing—it had been stolen. Can you imagine how angry she became? The idea of anyone stealing God's money! She even pronounced a curse on that person. Later, the thief turned out to be her own son, so she tried to appease everyone involved by begging him to take all this money and build some idols for his shrine. The son refused and passed the money back to his mother, who then went to the silversmith and gave him two hundred pieces of silver to build the idols. But there were eleven hundred pieces of silver originally. She gave two hundred pieces away and kept nine hundred pieces for herself!

FALSE SECURITY

This kind of reasoning is characteristic of those who love money. Such people always find God's money easier to keep than to give away. They think money can be trusted, but forget that *God alone is our security*. God is our source! How can any of us fail to be secure as a Christian when we realize that God is immensely more interested in our well-being than we are? Jesus said God even knows when a sparrow falls from the sky, and He reminded us that we are worth "far more than many sparrows" (Matthew 10:31).

Scripture says God never sleeps (Psalm 121:4). He is constantly aware of our needs. We are told that he knows our needs even before we ask, and while we are asking, the answer is on the way (Isaiah 65:24). The simplest understanding of the loving nature of our heavenly Father brings deep security to the believer. With that assurance, we can give His money without reservation or fear about the future.

Perhaps the woman in Micah's day had lived through hard times, like some of us. For whatever reason, she was holding on to nine hundred pieces of silver that she had said belonged to God. She needed to learn to walk by faith and not by sight, realizing, like the apostle Paul, that true contentment and inner happiness are not determined by outward circumstances. Paul said, "I have learned to be content in whatever circumstances I am" (Philippians 4:12, NASB). He knew his security was not in national economic prosperity or personal financial reserves, but in the Lord Jesus Christ alone!

Jesus said, "A man's life does not consist in the abundance of his possessions" (Luke 12:15, NIV). His emphasis when talking about material things was always upon the eternal and spiritual. "Lay not up for yourselves treasures upon earth . . . but lay up for yourselves treasures in heaven." (Matthew 6:20, NASB).

The Lord's teaching concerning security goes far beyond our immature, materialistic thinking, and touches on the true source of all security. Paul amplified this teaching on security when he stated confidently to the church at Philippi, "My God shall supply all your need according to His riches in glory by Christ Jesus" (Philippians 4:19). This is a promise, but it only becomes real to us when we claim it.

Christians who have not yet learned this blessed truth are happy and secure only so long as they have God's money in safekeeping to check on, to look at, and to think about. But the moment something happens to it, uncontrolled emotions break loose. The very idea of *losing* God's money! Then, if they get it back, they may fall in love with it again and are unwilling to part with even a small portion of it for His ministry.

I know a man who put a lot of money into stocks. When the market fell, he complained loudly about it because it prevented him from doing a "big" project for God. When stock market values later rose, this man still refused to sell out and do the "big deal" for God—even though he said all his stock belonged to God. Money was his security, and he loved it more than he was aware of or would admit.

I knew a banker who said he was a Christian, and who kept accumulating greater and greater assets throughout his entire business life. Even after a heart attack slowed him down some ten years before he died, he refused to part with much of God's money. Only after his death did anyone receive the benefit of the financial resources which God had entrusted to his care. He thus received little joy in his giving, even though he could have been a good example and a blessing to many. Unfortunately, his lifestyle became a stumbling block to some young men who admired his sharp business decisions but who made the mistake of adopting his materialistic value system.

Another wealthy Christian man I knew was a "workaholic" who amassed millions. For him, money meant power. He didn't make money to live, but lived to make money. He never really experienced the consistent joy of giving. When he did give, it was usually to projects that bore his name.

Although making money was his life, he was not interested in what happened to it after he was dead and gone. He left most of it to be controlled by a small board. The trustees are good people, but to my knowledge there is no indication that any of his funds are being used to fulfill the Great Commission. This board, like many others, probably does not understand that God wants the money He gives us to be used primarily to win the world for Christ.

Jesus Christ's main objective in dying on the cross was to fill heaven with redeemed people. He became a man and died and rose from the dead on the third day for that purpose. His resurrection proved He was God in the flesh, with all the resources needed to complete His program of world evangelization.

47

Yet in spite of this tremendous provision, the task of world evangelization has not been completed. Why? Among other reasons, massive quantities of God's funds have been misappropriated by His children. Today we continue to spend God's money on ourselves, rather than on the Great Commission. His goal has not become our goal. We do not yearn to redeem the lost as He does.

Not only does the Bible give us principles on how we should give, but it also warns us about holding on to what we have.

IS MONEY OUR IDOL?

How we handle our money is an accurate indicator of our spiritual lives. The Bible has much to say about what riches will do to us if money becomes our idol. The love of money may be Satan's most deceptive tactic. It can stunt our spiritual growth and cause us to become stumbling blocks to other Christians who are seeking victory in their own lives.

Scripture gives us numerous warnings that wealth can be here today and gone tomorrow. Job said that though a wicked man "heaps up silver like dust and clothes like piles of clay . . . when he opens his eyes, all is gone" (Job 27:16-19, NIV). And the psalmist said, "Proud man! Frail as breath! A shadow! And all his busy rushing ends in nothing. He heaps up riches for some-one else to spend" (Psalm 39:5-6, *Living Bible*).

I am haunted by the memory of what happened to one good friend of mine. His only daughter married a man who entered the oil business primarily with his wife's money. Later, the wife's parents tranferred a large portion of their assets to this couple in order to avoid inheritance taxes. With this rapid increase in wealth, the husband began to travel widely and to operate on a large scale. He became infatuated with another woman. His wife found out about it and divorced him. In the settlement he ended up with more than half of *her family's* resources, and her parents—who really made most of the money—are living out their days with barely enough money to live on.

The point of this illustration is simple. It is a foolish individual who sacrifices and saves and hoards God's money as though it were his own for the purpose of turning it over to a stranger to squander and spend. God will hold us accountable for what we do with His money.

THE MISUSE OF WEALTH

We have already seen that God is our source and that we must spend time with Him in order to learn how to give wisely. Now we will look at some passages containing significant warnings regarding the *misuse of wealth*— that is, holding on to what we have—and what God has to say about the disappointment of riches. "There is a grievous evil which I have seen under the sun: riches being hoarded by their owner to his hurt" (Ecclesiastes 5:13, NASB).

We normally think that attaining wealth is always good. We seldom consider that wealth can actually harm us. Yet Jesus in Luke 12:16-21 spoke about a greedy attitude produced by wealth in His piercing parable of the wealthy man who continued storing up things for himself to the very day of his death, but was not rich toward God.

Hoarding is a habit. We begin by grasping little things. Then we develop an appetite for more and more of this world's goods. Someone once asked John D. Rockefeller the question, "How many millions does it take to satisfy a man?" His candid answer accurately revealed the heart of man. He said, "The next one."

God warns us in advance about certain snares and traps along the way. Such a warning occurs in Deuteronomy 8 just before Israel is to possess the land God has promised them. God tells the people through Moses that He will bring them into a good land of plentiful water and fountains that spring out of the valleys and hills. It will be a land of wheat and barley, vines and fig trees, oil and honey. It will lack nothing.

Then comes the warning:

> Be careful that you do not forget the Lord your God, failing to observe His commands. . . . Otherwise, when you eat and are satisfied, when you build fine houses and settle down, and when your herds and flocks grow large and your silver and gold increase and all you have is multiplied, then your heart will become proud and you will forget the Lord your God. . . . You may say to yourself, "My power and the strength of my

hands have produced this wealth for me." But remember the Lord your God, for it is He who gives you the ability to produce wealth." (Deuteronomy 8:11-18, NIV)

I was closely associated with a godly Christian man in Texas who at middle age had a cash flow and assets sufficient to last him a lifetime. For many years this man had been giving abundantly to Christian causes. He also had been active in leading men to Christ and in helping them grow. One day he called several Christian friends together for lunch and proposed that we join together in a real estate development business in which most of the profits would go toward important Christian projects. He had located a choice tract of land and had a tentative contract to buy this property for a reasonable price. The seller wanted his money in five equal yearly installments, plus interest on the unpaid balance.

After we sold only fifty percent of the stock in the newly formed corporation, the investment looked so good that our associate recommended we keep the other half. But within a year after starting the new venture, house building for the entire city fell from six hundred homes per year to two hundred. Problems on top of problems continued to come our way. Each year when the payment and interest were due, only a miracle from God provided the necessary cash to keep this venture afloat.

After sixteen years without a single dividend being

51

paid, the venture began to show a glimmer of light at the end of the tunnel. But during all this time, the man who first proposed the business had gone through turmoil day after day. He had suffered a severe heart attack, had no time for outreach in winning the lost to Christ, and had little money available to give to God. Two years before our venture finally began to succeed, the man found personal victory and admitted to several on the board of directors that he did not get into this deal for the purpose he told us. His main objective was to make lots of money and be recognized as an astute business-man.

When the business later was earning enough profit to begin paying dividends, he suffered a second heart at-tack and died before reaching the hospital.

Any of us can be lured by the love of fame and for-tune to make decisions without waiting for the full ap-proval of God. Let's beware of trying to "help out poor old God." He's not looking for our help. What he desires is our obedience.

A second danger revealed in Deuteronomy 8 is the sin of idolatry. Once a man forgets God, he begins to be proud of his financial accomplishments and to worship the things money will buy. In the time of Moses, those who fell into this trap met a bitter end, for the Scripture says, "If you ever forget the Lord your God, and follow other gods, and worship and bow down to them, I testify against you today that you will surely be destroyed" (Deuteronomy 8:19, NIV).

In subsequent years, when many of the people did perish due to God's judgment, Israel could always look back to this clear and unmistakable prior warning from God.

God's judgment should never come to us as a surprise. He always lovingly instructs us in the path that is in our best interest and which will bring us the greatest happiness in life. His warnings against idolatry are not motivated by any need of His but rather because He knows what will truly make us happy. When He says, "Thou shalt worship the Lord thy God and Him only shalt thou serve," His interest is not self-serving, for He knows that our greatest joy lies in loving and worshiping Him. Therefore, for our good, He instructs us to put Him first in all things, and this includes how we use our money.

In Acts 5 we see the same warning underscored again. Barnabas, a godly layman from the island of Cyprus and known for his encouraging spirit, sold a tract of land and gave the full sale price as a love gift to the Lord. At the same time, a couple named Ananias and Sapphira sold a piece of land. It appears that they wanted to make a gift to God like Barnabas. But they loved money so much they were deceitful about their gift, and while professing to give it all, they kept part of it for themselves. The apostle Peter said to Ananias, "Why has Satan filled your heart to lie to the Holy Spirit and keep back part of the price of the land for yourself? While it remained, was it not your own? And after it was

53

sold, was it not in your control? Why have you conceived this thing in your heart? You have not lied to men but to God" (Acts 5:3-4, *The New King James Bible*). As a result of the sin of idolatry, God's judgment came into the lives of this couple: "And Ananias, hearing these words, fell down and breathed his last." Only three hours later God slew his wife as well for this sin.

<u>We become guilty of idolatry by adoring or worshiping anything that comes between us and God or that places God in second place in our lives.</u>

We cannot escape the Bible's warnings by ignoring them. God created spiritual laws to be as dependable and operative as His physical laws. His warnings are much like gravity—ignoring them in no way affects the way they function. When we break God's rules, which were set in motion for our good, we pay the price. Therefore, it is imperative that every Christian be instructed in how to handle money in accordance with God's will.

All around us we see the fruits of disobedience to these warnings—excessive drinking, drug addiction, immorality, broken homes, proud spirits, self-centered lives, illnesses of all kinds, suicides. When we fail to believe and live out the truth that *God is our source*, we deny that He is the one who has given us the power to accumulate wealth.

Consequently, we fail to practice biblical principles of giving and go down to spiritual defeat day after day and year after year.

THE DISAPPOINTMENT OF RICHES

Most people grow up having a desire to become rich. They fail to realize what the Bible says about *the disappointment of riches*.

God sometimes opens up to us Scriptures that become turning points in our lives. These are times when a biblical truth becomes practical and gives answers to real problems in our Christian experience. One passage that spoke to me in this way is the story of the rich young ruler:

> And as He was setting out on a journey, a man ran up to Him and knelt before Him and began asking Him, "Good Teacher, what shall I do to inherit eternal life?" And Jesus said to him, "Why do you call Me good? No one is good except God alone. You know the commandments, 'Do not murder, Do not commit adultery, Do not steal, Do not bear false witness, Do not defraud, Honor your father and mother.'" And he said to Him, "Teacher, I have kept all these things from my youth up." And looking at him, Jesus felt a love for him, and said to him, "One thing you lack: go and sell all you possess, and give to the poor, and you shall have treasure in heaven; and come, follow Me." But at these words his face fell, and he went away grieved, for he was one who owned much property.
>
> And Jesus, looking around, said to His disciples, "How hard it will be for those who are wealthy to enter the kingdom of God!" And the disciples were amazed

at His words. But Jesus answered again and said to them, "Children, how hard it is to enter the kingdom of God! It is easier for a camel to go through the eye of a needle than for a rich man to enter the kingdom of God." And they were even more astonished and said to Him, "Then who can be saved?" Looking upon them, Jesus said, "With men it is impossible, but not with God; for all things are possible with God." (Mark 10:17-27, NASB)

Jesus did not mean that a rich man who will sell all he has and give to the poor will consequently go to heaven. Salvation is never earned by divesting oneself of all one's possessions. However, this young man had a deep problem—*that of loving his money*. He was more devoted to his possessions than to God. Every man, rich or poor, must love God above possessions (or anything else in his life) if he desires to enter the kingdom of God.

But the "natural man" does *not* love God supremely. That is why Jesus gave an illustration of something that is impossible. He was saying that a man must be *perfect* to get to heaven, which is an impossibility, humanly speaking.

It is impossible to put a full-grown desert camel through the eye of a sewing needle. It is just as impossible for a rich man—a man in love with his money to the extent that he puts that money above all else, particularly Jesus Christ—to go to heaven. The man who trusts in riches in this instance is one who has an attitude which says, "This money is *mine*! I would rather have my money than Jesus Christ." This type of man is actually demonstrating the sinfulness of his heart and proving that "all have sinned and come short of the glory of God" (Romans 3:23). If this sin alone (loving money more than God) can keep an otherwise righteous man out of heaven, think of the spiritual damage it can cause in the life of a Christian who clings to his money.

Jesus did not say it is wrong to be wealthy. The problem is putting wealth *above* all else. Money is neither good nor bad; it is amoral. The sin consists in what the owner of money allows it to do to his heart. Actual possession of wealth may have little to do with "loving money." A poor man can be just as guilty as a rich man when he loves his meager possessions more than God.

But God can change a man's heart. Jesus concluded this lesson on giving and salvation by saying that with men, salvation is impossible, but not with God; for with God all things are possible. Despite man's sinful heart which keeps him out of heaven, God is able by his grace, through our faith in Jesus Christ, to provide the perfect righteousness His holiness demands.

Years ago one of the world's wealthiest men heard Billy Graham deliver a challenging message on the supremacy of Christ. Being deeply convicted by the Spirit of God, this man said to Dr. Graham, "I would give everything I own in exchange for the peace and assurance you possess." Dr. Graham replied, "You can have salvation for nothing, but you cannot receive it in exchange for something. I know you would be willing to give any material possession to buy it, but that would be impossible. Only Christ could purchase salvation on our behalf, and this He did by giving His life on the cross."

When Jesus said, "For with God all things are possible," He was well aware that He was headed toward Calvary, where the impossible—righteous standing before God for unrighteous man—would be accomplished and made available to all who believe. One can almost feel the depth of His disappointment when the rich young ruler walked away.

In another situation Jesus told His audience, "Beware, and be on your guard against every form of greed; for not even when one has an abundance does his life consist of his possessions" (Luke 12:15, NASB). This greed means a desire to have more and more, and it leads to taking advantage of or defrauding other people for gain.

Jesus continued in Luke 12:16-21 to illustrate the futility of amassing and storing great wealth.

> And He told them a parable, saying, "The land of a certain rich man was very productive. And he began reasoning to himself, saying, 'What shall I do, since I have no place to store my crops?' And he said, 'This is what I will do: I will tear down my barns and build larger ones, and there I will store all my grain and my goods. And I will say to my soul, "Soul, you have many goods laid up for many years to come; take your ease,

eat, drink and be merry.'" But God said to him, 'You fool! This very night your soul is required of you; and now who will own what you have prepared?' So is the man who lays up treasure for himself, and is not rich toward God." (NASB)

The warnings are self-explanatory. You will note this time that we have a "certain rich man" who "began reasoning to himself." It is evident the man did not pray to God for direction about how to conserve his riches. His personal decision was to build bigger and bigger barns for himself. These decisions promoted his own selfish comfort, which is the exact opposite of a Christ-centered attitude.

I knew a man who spent his whole life building one fortune after another. He had little time to enjoy life, because he was always working on a new business opportunity to make more money. He literally built larger barns in which to store his goods. His giving to the Lord was limited, and his vision for winning souls for Christ was small. He never let himself think in that direction.

I tried many times to get him involved in Bible study and in going to meetings where the speakers would effectively expound the word of God. His answer to me was always the same: "I am satisfied with what I am doing. Even if I knew more, I would not change now. Later I plan to sell out my business and then go full-time for the Lord." This man died before he sold any of his properties.

Many new Christians begin their pilgrimage still having the attitude that making and spending money is not a part of the Christian life. But when they received Christ as Savior they were giving Him a title deed to every hour of their day and every possession. This is what "lordship" means. When Christ died on the cross to purchase us and free us from the penalty of sin, He redeemed not only our spirits, but everything in our lives— including finances.

PRAY ABOUT FINANCIAL DECISIONS

Therefore, all of our decisions must be based on the will of God. Every financial decision must be prayerfully made on that basis alone. Many astute business people never pray about the deals they are making, even though they pray about every other area of their lives. They have never fully comprehended that everything they own is actually God's and should therefore be subject to His leadership.

I once heard of a Christian man who very honestly said, "Over the years since I was saved I have never prayed for money. I never pray about business deals, because I do not want God to think I am trying to use Him in some way to get Him to bless me in making money." This dear man's comments probably represent the feeling of thousands of businessmen who do not yet fully understand the biblical principle of God's ownership. They do not recognize that God's desire for their lives may include enabling them to make money in order to support His worldwide plan for evangelism. If they understand that He owns everything, they would immediately begin asking Him for specific guidance in order to make good investments and to increase the resources available for *His* purposes. They would no longer think it selfish to ask for His guidance, for they would understand that this is exactly what God earnestly desires.

The trouble with the rich man in Jesus' parable is that he made money an end in itself. He did not want to use it. He wanted to store it. Many people are like this foolish man. They are storing up things they will never get around to using.

A CHANNEL, NOT A STOREHOUSE

The picture of stewardship in the New Testament church is that of being channels of blessing to others rather than keepers of a storehouse. Perhaps this is why nothing is said about endowments and great programs for assuring the ongoing of the early church. Christians were not storehouses, but dynamic examples of giving and serving to the people of their day. Perhaps no character quality so marked the presence of Christ in their lives as did their attitude toward giving:

> And the congregation of those who believed were of one heart and soul; and not one of them claimed that anything belonging to him was his own. . . . There was not a needy person among them, for all who were

61

owners of land or houses would sell them and bring
the proceeds of the sales, and lay them at the apostles'
feet; and they would be distributed to each, as any had
need. (Acts 4:32-35, NASB)

This caring attitude toward the truly needy is a missing
note in many churches of this day.

Such dedication and unselfishness enabled God to
pour out His Spirit and blessings upon their lives in an
unprecedented manner. Perhaps the hindrance to the
great revival that so many of us yearn to see is our sin of
selfishness. The first commandment is "Love God with
all your heart," but Jesus gave a new commandment
recorded in John 13:34—"Love one another as I have
loved you." The depth of this love can be appreciated
only in the light of what Jesus was willing to give—everything!

God has exciting plans for all of us if only we will
stop chasing the dollar and see life from His perspective.
The One who created us wants to continue revealing
Himself to us so we can live our lives more abundantly
day by day. Jesus said, "I am come that they might have
life, and that they might have it more abundantly" (John
10:10).

One of the greatest hindrances to a giving lifestyle is
that so many people procrastinate—they are always
waiting to get started. Someone has aptly defined procrastination as "suicide on the installment plan."

I was visiting with my pastor one day and found him

depressed. He told me that his thirteen-year-old son was on the school's track team and had been working out for several months on the 440-yard dash. But now in a citywide competition the boy had to run unexpectedly in a race of only 330 yards, and he had not done well. As he explained it to his father, "I started my sprint too late, since I was saving my energy, and the race was over too soon. I had too much energy left."

The race of life is often run the same way. Many people say they are saving money until just the right time to give it away, but far too often the race is ended and they have too much left over. They started their "sprint" too late. The race of life was shorter than they expected, and God's money was never used for His purpose. This is why God teaches us to give money as we make it.

Another problem we have, one that is related to procrastination, is plain old stinginess. Solomon warned against the "stingy" life: "One man gives freely yet gains even more. Another withholds unduly, but comes to poverty. A generous man will prosper; he who refreshes others will himself be refreshed" (Proverbs 11:24-25, NIV). Some people never plan to give, like the stingy man in this proverb. Frequently, however, the problem with Christians is more subtle. We talk about our plans to give but never get around to giving. The man who is always saving for just the right "big project" usually knows little about how to interpret what God wants him to do. His worldly conversation and double-minded lifestyle reveal his low level of spiritual maturity.

I once knew a man who formed a foundation in which to store his money. The foundation kept increasing its assets for years. As I talked with him regarding his giving, he remarked, "I never seem to find enough good projects to spend the money on."

What a tragedy it is that people in his own city, state, nation, and world were dying without Christ in great numbers, yet he could not find a project for which to use God's money. Such a man has no vision—he cannot see things from God's point of view.

THREE GUIDELINES

For every disappointment which material possessions may bring, there is a positive solution pointed out in the Bible. When properly understood and properly managed, riches can provide much joy and be the means of accomplishing a great deal of essential ministry in the cause of Christ.

First, we must guard our hearts against "the love of riches." Solomon, an extremely wealthy man, once said, "Above all else, guard your affections. For they influence everything else in your life" (Proverbs 4:23, *Living Bible*).

Jesus spoke to this matter in Matthew 6:33: "Seek ye first the kingdom of God, and His righteousness; and all these things shall be added unto you." When our hearts are in love with the things that God is in love with, money will be no problem, and riches will not become a disappointment in our lives.

On this matter of the heart's affection, Paul's word to the Christians of Colosse is most instructive: "If ye then be risen with Christ, seek those things which are above, where Christ sitteth on the right hand of God. Set your affection on things above, not on things on the earth" (Colossians 3:1-2). This kind of mindset will result in *sacrificial giving* rather than just big talk.

Second, we must be careful to do our giving for the right reason.

Take care! Don't do your good deeds publicly, to be admired, for then you will lose the reward from your Father in heaven. When you give a gift to a beggar, don't shout about it as the hypocrites do—blowing trumpets in the synagogues and streets to call attention to their acts of charity! I tell you in all earnestness, they have received all the reward they will ever get. But when you do a kindness to someone, do it secretly —don't tell your left hand what your right hand is doing. And your Father who knows all secrets will reward you." (Matthew 6:1-4, *Living Bible*)

Riches given for the wrong reason will bring great disappointment to the donor because the act of giving will have no eternal consequences. The apostle John's comment summarizes why some people make a proud display of gifts: "They loved the praise of men more than the praise of God" (John 12:43).

Third, we must make giving our primary objective in obtaining wealth. The writer of Proverbs said, "Do

65

not weary yourself to gain wealth; cease from your consideration of it. When you set your eyes on it, it is gone. For wealth certainly makes itself wings, like an eagle that flies toward the heavens" (Proverbs 23:4-5, NASB).

Wealth is meant to be given. When one attempts to possess it and cling to it, he finds to his deep disappointment that it flies away. A fire, a lawsuit, a depression, inflation, illness, divorce, wayward children, and a host of other familiar problems are the enemies of wealth. Giving is the friend of wealth, for with it comes joy and fulfillment rather than disappointment.

Both eventualities are pictured in Proverbs 11:28—"Whoever trusts in his riches will fall, but the righteous will thrive like a green leaf" (NIV).

Three simple guidelines are: Guard your hearts against the love of riches; be careful to give for the right reason; and make giving a primary objective in obtaining wealth. These guidelines are enough to change a person's life.

Chapter SIX

A MOUNTAIN OF GIVING

In my study of giving as worship I was astonished at how this principle is illustrated in the life of King David.

Perhaps no individual in the Old Testament came from a more humble beginning than the shepherd boy named David, the youngest in a family of eight boys. Yet no one in the Bible ever gave as large a financial gift to the work of God as did this one man. His life was climaxed by a "mountain" of giving.

David's son Solomon usually receives credit in our minds for being the builder of the temple. But it was David who gathered and gave all the building materials, including the gold, silver and precious stones, to construct the temple. David had wanted to build the Lord's

temple himself (1 Chronicles 22:7-8), but God allowed him only the privilege of giving to help make it possible. He said, "Now with all my ability I have provided for the house of my God the gold . . . silver . . . bronze . . . iron . . . wood . . . onyx and inlaid stones, stones of antimony, and stones of various colors, and all kinds of precious stones, and alabaster in abundance" (1 Chronicles 29:2, NASB). When he also said he had prepared for the Lord's house "with great pains" (1 Chronicles 22:14, NASB), he meant that giving did not come easily. The preparation took hard work and more than twenty years of determination.

DAVID'S PRAISE TO GOD

David's example was followed by the tribal, military, and royal officials of Israel, who also gave "willingly" and "with perfect heart" (1 Chronicles 29:9) to the project of building the temple. After this, David praised the Lord in the presence of the whole assembly:

> Blessed art Thou, O Lord God of Israel our father, forever and ever. Thine, O Lord, is the greatness and the power and the glory and the victory and the majesty, indeed everything that is in the heavens and the earth; Thine is the dominion, O Lord, and Thou dost exalt Thyself as head over all. Both riches and honor come from Thee, and Thou dost rule over all, and in Thy hand is power and might; and it lies in Thy hand to make great, and to strengthen everyone. Now therefore, our God, we thank Thee, and praise Thy glorious name.

But who am I and who are my people that we should
be able to offer as generously as this? For all things
come from Thee, and from Thy hand we have given
Thee. (1 Chronicles 29:10-14, NASB)

David realized something which most of us fail to
understand—all our gifts to God came from Him in the
first place. *God is our source.* For a shepherd boy to be
able to offer perhaps the largest financial gift any man
ever gave to God only reflects a deeper fact—that David
was truly a man "after God's own heart" (Acts 13:22).

Our very ability to give is a gift itself, and this was
true with David. As God saw that David was faithful in a
few little things, He made him ruler over many things.
Humanly speaking, it would have been utterly impossible for David to have made his gift for the temple
through any merit or ability of his own. But when God
saw that he was spiritually faithful and usable, He entrusted him with this enormous privilege and responsibility. The same God who dealt with David also deals
with us in this way today.

PRIOR COMMITMENTS

A number of years ago I was eating lunch with two other
men. Both of them were in the oil business and both had
their own airplanes. The day before, Joe had been flying
in from west Texas and was caught in a storm.

Jim said to him, "What did you do when you got in
the storm?"

"Well," said Joe, "I got pretty scared."

"Well, did you pray?"

"You know I prayed!"

"What did you tell the Lord?"

"I told Him if He would get me through this thing, I would do anything He wanted me to do."

"Well," said Jim, "obviously you made it—what are you going to do?"

"Oh, Jim, you know how that is."

"What do you mean?"

"You've made promises to the Lord like that. Did you keep them?"

"I sure did!"

"What kind of promises did you make?"

"I told Him if He would help me make my deal with Texaco I would give Him one third of all I ever made."

"Did you do that?"

"I sure did. I'm still doing it—and the deal is making more money every year!"

Out of curiosity, over the years I have watched that one deal Jim made and seen God bless it more and more.

The value of making prior commitments to God can be seen in every investment of money. Whether it is related to the income of a piece of property, the sale of an asset, or making a faith promise, the principle is the same. A prior commitment protects us from pressures and temptations which may come later, after the new income has become a reality or after the investment has become a success.

In the life of another person, a young seminary student with a very modest income, I saw God use this same principle in another way.

The young man's tithe was twenty dollars a month, and he and his wife had a great desire to be able to give more than that amount to the Lord's work. Because of that burden, they began to pray that God would show them a way in which they could have the privilege of giving more. As a result, the Lord inspired a song which they wrote in a few brief minutes. When the song was published, the young man made a commitment in prayer that none of the resources from that song would ever be used for any purpose other than giving to the Lord's work.

By the end of that first year, the seminary student's gifts were equal to his gross income from all other sources. By the end of sixteen years the song had been recorded by many Christian artists and was played over the air hundreds of times each month. All the royalties produced by the song were given to the Lord for the purpose of carrying out the Great Commission.

There are no limits to God's ability to answer prayer. If we want to give badly enough, He will show us a way.

Chapter SEVEN

PRACTICAL PRINCIPLES OF GIVING

Some serious thinking should give you the answer to a question implied in Jesus' teaching on riches: "Would you rather be wealthy for a few years on earth or wealthy for eternity in heaven?"

A wise person who wants to be eternally wealthy in heaven will make his plans accordingly.

PLAN TO BE RICH IN HEAVEN

A major motivation behind giving on earth is to store up treasures in heaven. Again, recall that Jesus declared, "Do not store up for yourselves treasures on earth, where moth and rust destroy, and where thieves break in and steal. But store up for yourselves treasures in heaven. . . . For where your treasure is, there your heart will be also" (Matthew 6:19-21, NIV).

One night a little girl asked her father about this, saying, "Daddy, how do you get your money up to God in heaven?" The father replied, "Sweetheart, you can't send physical dollars to heaven, but you can give your money to help save people so they can go to be with God forever. That's how you can get your riches up to heaven—they can only go there through the people who are helped spiritually by your gifts."

If you really want to know where your heart is, look back over your canceled checks for the last three years and see where your money has gone. This exercise may reveal more than you want to know! How much of your money is actually being stored up in heaven?

It is so easy to spend money on things we love here and now. Alcoholics are eager to spend their last dollar on whiskey. "Shopaholics" compulsively spend countless dollars on unneeded merchandise, rather than prayerfully seeking to make wise investments. I was visiting with an unhappy husband one afternoon who told me his wife spent all her time shopping—not only shopping, but buying. "What kind of things does she buy?" I asked. He replied, "In her closet right now there are more than forty pairs of beautiful shoes—many of which are still in the boxes and have never been worn!"

An honest look at our lives will reveal whether we are living according to Colossians 3:2—"Set your affection on things above, not on things on the earth."

No matter what the affections of your heart may be, your checkbook will reveal them to you. <u>Spending money unwisely may be foolish, but spending God's money without His consent is sin</u>. Sooner or later, such a lifestyle will undermine our testimony for Christ and will adversely affect the quality of our lives.

Satan is eager to accommodate our fleshly desires and will provide moths, rust, and thieves in abundance to help dissipate and consume as much of God's money as possible. So resist Satan and invest your money in the safest place in the universe: heaven.

GIVE TO THOSE WHO MINISTER TO YOU

We should support financially those who minister the word of God to us, as Paul pointed out in 1 Corinthians 9:14—"The Lord directed those who proclaim the gospel to get their living from the gospel" (see 1 Corinthians 9:7-14).

Jesus, in sending out the seventy, told them to depend for a living on those to whom they preached: "Stay on at the same house eating and drinking what they provide, for the workman deserves his support" (Luke 10:7, *Williams*). Although that was a special commission, the principle remains true for our age. This principle is stated by Paul in another letter: "Those who are taught the truth should share all their goods with the man who teaches them" (Galatians 6:6, *Williams*). One of the main reasons my wife and I support our church is because they teach us the word of God.

75

PLAN FOR A SHORT LIFE

We are, in the language of a friend from Texas, "tenant farmers with a short-term lease!" Job said, "My days are swifter than a weaver's shuttle" (Job 7:6, NASB). And the apostle James wrote, "You do not know what your life will be like tomorrow. You are just a vapor that appears for a little while and then vanishes away" (James 4:14, NASB). The brevity of life inspired Moses to write these words: "So teach us to number our days that we may apply our hearts unto wisdom" (Psalm 90:12).

A highly productive businessman who has been a close friend of mine for many years once calculated the number of days he had left if he should be privileged to live to the age of seventy. To remind him to live each day to the fullest and not become spiritually complacent, each day he subtracts one from that total number of days he expects to live.

The person who plans to live each day to the fullest lives wisely. He will not leave things undone because of procrastination. He will seek to live one day at a time and get the most out of life.

"Redeeming the time" (Ephesians 5:16) is a practice the Lord commands because a spiritual battle is in progress, and every day we are moving closer to His appearing in glory. As evangelist Grady Wilson frequently says, "Whatever we are going to do for God, we had best do quickly."

No life so perfectly portrays this principle as that of Christ Himself. He was constantly making preparations to leave. He anticipated a brief life and spoke frequently of the time when He would again be with His Father. In His triumphant prayer He said, "I have glorified Thee on the earth; I have finished the work which Thou gavest Me to do" (John 17:4). <u>Once a man understands that God has actually given a job for him to do and only a few years in which to do it, he will be willing to burn out to accomplish that mission.</u>

For both Christ and Paul, heaven was near and always in their thinking. Their idea of success was to complete their mission and go home to the Father. In the last paragraphs of Paul's last epistle, he expressed his feeling of victory with these words: "I have fought the good fight, I have finished the course, I have kept the faith; in the future there is laid up for me the crown of righteousness, which the Lord, the righteous Judge, will award to me on that day; and not only to me, but also to all who have loved His appearing" (2 Timothy 4:7-8, NASB).

MAKE CHRIST LORD OF ALL

Jesus once taught a parable which described four types of soil. One of the soil types contained thorns. After the seed of God's word had been planted in this soil, those thorns continued to grow unhindered. Their devastating effect is described by Jesus in His explanation of the parable. He described these thorns as "the worries of the world, and the deceitfulness of riches, and the desires for other things." Their terrible result in our

77

lives is that they "enter in and choke the word, and it becomes unfruitful" (Mark 4:19, NASB).

The Bible warns that a person can start out well and end up poorly! The truth Jesus is teaching regarding salvation in this parable applies to every area of our lives.

A person can hear what God has to say about giving and start out with excellent intentions. But when he encounters worries, financial temptations, and the constant allurement of "other things," his first love for Christ may be choked out, and he becomes mediocre in his spiritual commitment.

In my own voyage through life I have met many businessmen whose lives are "choked." They say they have made the wonderful discovery of knowing Jesus Christ personally, and for a time they appear to grow spiritually. Suddenly, without saying a word to anyone, they begin to go backward. When others talk about the Bible or Jesus Christ, they do not pursue the conversation. They have nothing current from their Bible reading or their ministry to talk about. Nor are they interested in what God may be doing spiritually in the lives of others. They seem to be more conversant about business, money matters, taxes, politics, sports and travel than with anything spiritual. They refuse to go to meetings where they might be challenged to renew their interest in Jesus Christ and His word. They will tell you, "I am satisfied with my life. I am not really interested in doing more spiritually than I am doing right now."

If we could look back over the spiritual history of

one of these Christians, we might well discover that he was progressing along the road to spiritual maturity until he was confronted with Christ's call to relinquish any claim on his *money*. Then he took a long, hard look at the possibility of losing this "idol," and refused to obey the Bible when it spoke about money. At this point of disobedience, he stopped growing spiritually! He may have been troubled at first, but eventually his conscience was hardened and he became satisfied with being a lukewarm Christian, the kind Jesus warns about in Revelation 3:15-16—"I know your deeds, that you are neither cold nor hot. I wish you were either one or the other! So, because you are lukewarm—neither hot nor cold—I am about to spit you out of my mouth" (NIV).

A lukewarm Christian is normally challenged more by business and social achievements than by serving God. Yet in a matter of a few years—or less time for some—he will have passed on into eternity, and the wealth he has so diligently accumulated will be lost or spent by others—sometimes not even by those he loved.

The fear of parting with money reminds me of a decision I made during my flying days. I was handicapped because I was unwilling to pay the price to learn to pilot a plane by instruments. Because of this refusal, I could never fly through the clouds. My highest altitude was always determined by the elevation of the cloud cover, so I stayed down where the air was often turbulent, the visibility poor, and collision with other planes a constant threat.

79

Many Christians are like that. They will not pay the price *now* in order to reap rich spiritual rewards on down the road. They start out by growing spiritually, and then come to the place where they need to part ownership with their pocketbooks. If they refuse to obey God here because this price seems too high, they will have reached the pinnacle of their Christian growth. They can never go higher than that "spiritual cloud level."

Some Christians have remained defeated for years because of financial idolatry. They should be mature Christians and servants of God, but instead they remain spiritual babes in the church. The words of Hebrews 5:12 are addressed to them: "Though by this time you ought to be teachers, you need someone to teach you the elementary truths of God's word all over again. You need milk, not solid food!" (Hebrews 5:12, NIV).

PLAN AHEAD TO GIVE

In 1 Corinthians 16:1-2 we learn that Christians should plan their giving ahead of time. "Now here are the directions about the money you are collecting to send to the Christians in Jerusalem (and by the way, these are the same directions I gave to the churches in Galatia). On every Lord's Day each of you should put aside something from what you have earned during the week, and use it for this offering. The amount depends on how much the Lord has helped you earn. Don't wait until I get there and then try to collect it all at once" (1 Corinthians 16:1-2, *Living Bible*).

These instructions are practical and easy to follow. Everyone was to participate and to do his giving prior to Paul's arrival.

GIVE TO YOUR CHURCH

These particular gifts in 1 Corinthians 16 were for a mission project. Today most of our gifts normally should go to a local church, provided that the church is preaching and applying the word of God in such a way that people are being saved, nourished, and instructed in the grace and knowledge of Christ.

The test of your feeling about the effectiveness of your church can be measured by your confidence and joy in giving. I know of a pastor who believes strongly that the local church is synonymous with the "storehouse" in the Old Testament, and who said, "All the tithe should be given to the Lord through the local church." The man he was talking with said, "For years, I was a member of a church in a denomination where many of its pastors did not aggressively preach the word of God, had no evangelistic zeal, and substituted social action for mission. Very few adults found Christ in our worship services or found good nourishment for their spiritual growth. Are you saying I should have been giving my tithe to that church?"

The pastor paused thoughtfully, then replied, "No, if they are not preaching God's word and being true to the Scriptures, I have no basis to really encourage you to give them your tithe."

81

INVEST IN PEOPLE

People were Jesus' first concern. He gave Himself not for an insitution, but for *people* of every kind and background. How can we follow his example in ministering through giving today? And how does this giving relate to storing up riches in heaven?

When we give to feed the poor, we are sharing a *testimony of the love of God* which can eventually open the door for us to share the gospel. Regardless of where God leads us to give, our objective should be not only to meet the immediate need but to save individual souls for eternity.

While it is a great privilege to be able to feed starving people physically, it is even better to teach them how to feed themselves spiritually. Having first demonstrated visibly the love of Christ, we can then share the gospel with them. The ultimate goal, of course, is to bring them to the saving knowledge of Christ our Savior. Jesus underscored the preeminence of the spiritual need of man in Matthew 4:4 when He quoted this Old Testament Scripture: "Man shall not live by bread alone, but by every word that proceedeth out of the mouth of God."

LET GOD LEAD YOU

A consecrated believer, living under the control of the Spirit of God, will find direction from God regarding all his giving—the amount of the gifts and who should receive them. The scriptural guidelines in this book are intended to be only an outline. The Holy Spirit will fill in the outline as He speaks to you personally. When you seriously want to know *who* to give to and *how much*, remember to start with *prayer*. Beginning each morning with prayer and Bible reading with a personal application will provide guidance not only in giving but in other matters as well.

Recently a generous Christian couple came under the influence of a well-known religious leader. In his televised programs this leader placed a heavy emphasis on financial contributions. The couple had little knowledge of biblical principles of giving, had no daily devotional life, and were confronting at the time many personal problems. Impetuously they made a sizable gift to the religious leader's organization, though they knew little about its doctrine and integrity. As it turned out, the organization had nothing in common with this couple's true convictions. The television charisma and appeal swayed their judgment, and later they were sick at heart for having made the gift.

To carry out our good intentions we should develop realistic questions to ask those who request our gifts of God's resources. Good stewardship demands that we understand where and how the Lord's money is being used.

Recently, a representative of a religious group visited the home of a Christian and asked him to buy a record album for five dollars. The Christian asked the representative five simple questions about the organization he represented and about how their money was being used. These questions were:

1. Are they communicating a message true to the Scriptures?
2. Are people responding positively to the message?
3. Are the lives of the organization's leaders an illustration of the message?
4. Is the organization reproducing itself?
5. Is there a standard of excellence along with freedom from waste?

The representative listened to the questions, told the Christian goodby, and has never returned.

A WORD ABOUT ENDOWMENTS

Allow me here to share my convictions on the subject of "endowment" of organizations. We must be extremely careful in how we endow any Christian cause, be it church, program, or institution. There is enough history of endowed Christian institutions losing their true Christian focus to cause great alarm and caution in this area.

Many of America's earliest educational institutions came into being for the sole purpose of magnifying Jesus Christ and equipping missionaries and pastors to spread the gospel throughout the world. Through gifts and wills, these large institutions have been permanently endowed for many years. Today, however, they have long since lost their real zeal for evangelism and for teaching the word of God. Tragically, God's money continues to be tied up through endowments which support a theology foreign to the New Testament. The godly people who provided these funds were undoubtedly well intentioned, but they made very few requirements as to the use of their gifts.

I know of one organization that recently received endowment money which had been redirected from a theological seminary. For twenty years the seminary had benefitted from a well-written will, which includes a continuing requirement provision ("sliding endowment") to receive the funds. When the theological commitment of that seminary changed under the leadership of a new president, the school no longer qualified for the use of those endowment funds. This type of endowment is designed with safeguards to ensure that the continued wishes of the donor are carefully complied with.

Practically speaking, we can describe endowments in two ways. One is the traditional definition of "a permanent fund of provision for support." Usually such an endowment is based on a capital bequest in which only the capital's income or interest can be used for the purpose of ministry.

A second type of endowment can be thought of as a temporary endowment. This second approach to endowing a ministry is based on gifts of depreciating, income-producing assets, such as a rental property, oil or gas leases or overrides, or the royalties on a book or composition. Buildings decay, oil and gas wells deplete, and books go out of print or outlive their copyright, so none of these gifts provide a permanent endowment.

To the best of my knowledge, no institution which bases its major financial emphasis on current gifts and temporary endowments has ever become theologically unsound. The same cannot be said, however, for those which have majored on permanent endowments.

Another practical question relates to endowing a local congregation through wills or bequests. What might otherwise be a wonderful blessing to the church and to the Lord's work can be a spiritual tragedy if great care and wisdom are not used in this regard.

I know of two churches which received large gifts that were not wisely designated. In both cases, building payments and church operating expenses have received the proceeds of the endowments rather than missions, evangelism, scholarships, or the worthwhile benevolent ministries of the church. Both churches have gone downhill spiritually because their congregations have become stagnant in their faith and in their desire to give.

In another church, an endowment has been given which is more effective. The proceeds are designated to be used in a rotating fashion to assist missionary efforts and the education of seminary students. This church is continuing to trust God more and more for their ministries of evangelism and spiritual growth.

Endowments should contain the provision that if the recipient departs from the faith (and this "departure" must be carefully spelled out), then the endowment can be revoked and diverted to an organization or foundation that remains true to the word of God.

God has enough resources to complete all the work He wants done without our being financially independent, either personally or institutionally. The Bible teaches the principles upon which these works are supposed to be financed. Giving is a great joy, and tithing and making offerings are a great privilege and responsibility—but they must be done under the leadership of Christ. <u>The investment of a man's life and resources will be of no greater value than his ability and desire to listen to God.</u>

Chapter EIGHT

THE SECRET OF GIVING AS A LIFESTYLE

You may be wondering, "How can I get on my heart what God has on His heart?" Or you ask, "How can I accomplish a lifestyle of loving and giving as Jesus did?"

First, to have God's kind of lifestyle we must spend *time alone with God in a quiet place*. This time alone is *the secret of knowing the Lord:* "Cause me to hear Thy lovingkindness in the morning; for in Thee do I trust. Cause me to know the way wherein I should walk; for I lift up my soul unto Thee" (Psalm 143:8). Time alone with Him is indispensable if we want to appropriate the power available to us.

Andrew Murray wrote these paragraphs in his *Daily Secrets of Christian Living*:

Christ longed greatly that His disciples should know God as their Father, and that they should have secret fellowship with Him. In His own life He found it not only indispensable but the highest happiness to meet the Father in secret. And He would have us realize that it is impossible to be true, wholehearted disciples without daily conversation with the Father in heaven, who waits for us in secret.

God is a God who hides Himself from the world and all that is of the world. God would draw us away from the world and from ourselves. He offers us instead the blessedness of close, intimate communion with Himself. Oh, that God's children would understand this!

Believers in the Old Testament enjoyed this experience. "Thou art my hiding place." "He that dwelleth in the secret place of the Most High shall abide under the shadow of the Almighty." "The secret of the Lord is with them that fear him."

If the Old Testament saints found this "secret place of the most high" exhilarating, how much more ought New Testament Christians to enjoy their secret relationship with God. For "your life is hid with Christ in God" (Colossians 3:3). Our life, hidden with Christ in God, is safe and beyond the reach of every foe. We should each day confidently seek the renewal of this life through prayer to our Father who is in secret. The roots of our daily lives, like the roots of a tree hidden under the earth, are hidden deep in God.

But many Christians, even Christian leaders, do not have a devotional life. Dawson Trotman, the founder of The Navigators, used to say that most of the failures in the lives and ministries of Christian leaders could be traced to their lack of a consistent devotional life.

KEYS TO A SUCCESSFUL "QUIET TIME"

Consider these guidelines for making your daily "quiet time" with God a satisfying and God-honoring experience:

1. Our first thought in prayer should be: "I am alone with God and God is with me." We must wait on Him until we sense His presence, so that we may have His power and wisdom to live our lives in a manner pleasing to Him. "Be still and know that I am God" (Psalm 46:10). We must be silent before God, taking time to meditate on the wonderful revelation of God's love in Christ until we are filled with the spirit of worship and wonder and desire for God.

2. Take time to believe the precious truth that "the love of God is shed abroad in our hearts by the Holy Ghost who is given unto us" (Romans 5:5). Ask yourself how much you have believed in and sought after God's love.

3. As you pray, hold fast this assurance: "I am confident that my heavenly Father longs to manifest His love to me. I am deeply convinced of the truth that He will do it." Your prayers must be sincere.

Surrender your will to Him, and by faith expect
Him to furnish all you need to do His will today.

THE IMPORTANCE OF SPIRITUAL MATURITY

I recall how during a certain period of my life my lack of
spiritual growth and my ignorance of God's word allowed Satan to use me. I had been convicted by God to
sell my part of a corporation in which I had a small interest. The money from this sale was put into a foundation for giving to Christian works. I continued to main-
tain my interest in another business partnership. During
the next several years, my tax man, a "lukewarm" Christian, encouraged me to do all of my tithing and giving out
of the foundation funds and to use the total income from
my partnership for business and family expenses, and I
agreed.

There were times when I knew this procedure was
wrong. I felt that I should be giving God the tithe from my
business partnership too. I did begin to give a little
money from this source but not much.

Five years later I sold my interest in the partnership
properties. The sale price was far below what my evalua-
tion showed it should have been. I am convinced that,
due to my sin of failing to tithe this income for about five
years, the Lord permitted me to lose much more in this
sale than I had withheld from Him during those years. It
was a high price to pay for stealing from God.

Being alone with God on a daily basis can build increasing holiness and purity in your life, and will help

you avoid wrong decisions as you grow in your knowledge of the Lord, your experience of His grace, and your
obedience to His word.

Chapter NINE

GIVING OUT OF POVERTY

Many Christians do not know how to start giving because they are so pressed to pay daily bills they have nothing left. Their response to God's instructions on giving is like mine when my wife said we should tithe: "How can we tithe when we are spending more than we are making?" The answer now as then is, "I don't know how, but it works." There are many helpful books written on the subject of how to manage your personal finances, but the best place to start such management is to give the tithe first.

You don't have to possess large sums of money to be a "large giver." In his second letter to the Corinthians, Paul pointed out this example of the churches in

Macedonia: "In a great ordeal of affliction their abundance of joy and their deep poverty overflowed in the wealth of their liberality" (2 Corinthians 8:2, NASB).

A good many years ago, while slowly reading this passage, I recall thinking I must have misread the words. So I read them again: "In a great ordeal of affliction their abundance of joy *and their deep poverty* overflowed in the *wealth of their liberality*."

"Lord," I said, "there must be a mistake. Do You mean to say that when these people were in affliction and deep poverty they still 'overflowed' with liberal giving?" I admitted before the Lord that this was not my experience in giving, but prayed that if He would open to me what this passage meant and how I was to do it, I would give it a try.

I read on. Paul said, "I testify that according to their ability, and beyond their ability, they gave of their own accord" (verse 3). Then I realized these Christians had not given according to their natural abilities, but God had allowed them to give supernaturally, far above their natural power. Furthermore, they had done this willingly and voluntarily. No one had to twist their arms. They simply heard about the seriousness of the need, and gave spontaneously.

This kind of giving impressed me. I reread the passage and noticed especially the opening verse of this chapter: "Now, brethren, we wish to make known to you *the grace of God* which has been given in the churches of Macedonia." It had never occurred to me before that giving depended on *the grace of God*. This opened up a completely new concept. Giving is based on God's grace —God's *unmerited favor and power*. The Macedonian Christians had experienced that grace.

This "gracious" giving is joyful. Even though these people were experiencing "a great ordeal of affliction" —torture, torment, discomfort, and pain—they experienced inwardly the *abundance* of joy. Furthermore, they were in "deep poverty," with little or no income to give away. Yet they continued to give more and more until Paul could call it *liberal* or *lavish* giving.

Only God can accomplish this kind of giving, for *He is our source!*

These people had a desire to give, so they gave first what they could—"according to their ability" (verse 3). Then God's Spirit made it possible for them to give far beyond their own power—"beyond their ability." And they did this voluntarily—there was no forcing, no arm-twisting, no playing on their emotions. God controlled their wills. They *first* gave what *they* could; then God gave through them what *He* wanted them to give supernaturally. This had to be "giving" by the power of God.

Furthermore, we read Paul's testimony in verse 4 that these Macedonians were "begging us with much entreaty for the favor of participation in the support of the saints." In the *New International Version* this is translated, "They urgently pleaded with us for the privilege of sharing in this service to the saints." Isn't that tremendous? I saw that I could have fellowship with

97

another Christian *by giving to his material needs*! I saw that God is interested in *all* of my life, not just what I had thought of as a "spiritual" ministry.

Then I asked God, "How do I get this kind of desire to participate in giving? Give me whatever I need to be the kind of Christian who will beg to be financially involved in God-anointed ministries."

Then I read in verse 5 that the Macedonians "first gave themselves to the Lord." When we make the decision to make Christ Lord of our life, one of the first indications will be *the change which comes in our giving*. A whole new dimension of abundant giving will open up for our enjoyment.

For various reasons, the reality of total commitment does not normally come at the time of a person's conversion, although ideally it should. For Frances and me, this understanding and decision did not come until we had been married more than twenty years.

Looking back at this passage I found that the Macedonians, in spite of their affliction and poverty, had a real celebration of giving—they "*overflowed* in the wealth of their liberality."

We find here, then, that:

1. They gave sacrificially—"beyond their ability."
2. They gave willingly—"of their own accord."
3. They gave eagerly—"begging us with much entreaty."
4. They gave spiritually—"they first gave themselves to the Lord."

I have never known a pastor or layman to report that people begged him to take their money and give it away. There is a reason, however, why Paul's experience was different. His life of selflessness and love for others, as well as his love for Christ and His word, provided an example for the Macedonians and gave them the confidence that he would use the money far better than they could.

This "pacesetting" concept is implicit in Paul's earlier letter to the church at Thessalonica, which was one of the Macedonian churches, and it is a crucial concept for the Christian leader.

> As apostles of Christ we could have been a burden to you, but we were gentle among you, like a mother caring for her little children. We loved you so much that we were delighted to share with you not only the gospel of God but our lives as well, because you had become so dear to us. . . . You are witnesses, and so is God, of how holy, righteous and blameless we were among you who believed. For you know that we dealt with each of you as a father deals with his own children. (1 Thessalonians 2:7-11, NIV)

The Thessalonians saw in Paul's lifestyle the embodiment of his message. Many people had responded to his continual preaching of the gospel, and the church had seen before their eyes the lives of people changed from hate to love, from greed to giving, from darkness to light. Paul had even earned his own living by tentmaking so they would know that his interest in them was not for personal financial gain. The result was that the people trusted Paul. He lived out God's love, and this love was visible in his life.

This giving lifestyle should be our own deepest desire. Do you think it is possible? It is, but the price is high: unreserved yieldedness to the Lord Jesus Christ. If you feel you cannot pay this price, remember that he is not asking you for what is naturally possible. Here again, *God is our source.* He has made a way to provide *His* resources to us to use for His glory. Even in our act of surrender He helps us!

TOTAL COMMITMENT

Just as Paul noted that the Corinthians "first gave themselves to the Lord," so he also made a similar strong appeal to the Romans for total consecration: "I urge you therefore, brethren, by the mercies of God, to present your bodies a living and holy sacrifice, acceptable to God, which is your spiritual service of worship" (Romans 12:1, NASB).

What are the "mercies of God"? In context they are all of the gracious gifts of a sovereign God to undeserving sinners. Paul has dwelt on these "mercies" in the first eleven chapters of Romans, where he describes God's mercy—his pity and compassion for us. God's mercy has always been the great motivating force for our worship and service.

God's mercy was on David's mind, for example,

when he came to worship: "But I, by Your great mercy, will come into Your house; in reverence will I bow down toward Your holy temple" (Psalm 5:7, NIV). David recognized that he did not come to the Lord's house because he was worthy to come. We, like David, can also come to God by faith, because His mercy is greater than the multitude of our sins.

Mercy is also love. If I am in suffering and need, mercy appears as God's gift of love to help me, even though I am unworthy. Mercy is the expression of God's love, and love always *gives*. He has enough mercy to meet my every need—even my need for strength and wisdom to minister to others.

God is a giving Father because He is a loving Father. But like all lovers, God longs for a response from us. And Scripture indicates that our proper response will often come in the form of ministry to others, just as God has ministered to us.

Paul expresses it this way:

Praise be to the God and Father of our Lord Jesus Christ, the Father of compassion and the God of all comfort, who comforts us in all our troubles, so that we can comfort those in any trouble with the comfort we ourselves have received from God. (2 Corinthians 1:3-4, NIV)

Some years ago, Billie Hanks, Jr., president of International Evangelism Association, and Bob O'Brien, editor of the Baptist Press, were involved in a citywide crusade in Monrovia, Liberia. Toward the end of the crusade they had the opportunity to visit a mission ministry deep in the Liberian jungle. When they arrived they met four German Baptist missionary nurses who had dedicated the last fourteen years of their lives to minister to about forty thousand patients per year in a small out-patient clinic. Why were these women willing to give their lives and their love to strangers from a different culture and a different race? They comforted others because they had first been comforted by God.

As their story was related to me, Bob O'Brien remembered seeing a small child with lockjaw being tenderly fed mother's milk through a plastic tube. The Muslim father standing nearby showed signs of great relief as the child responded to the milk. Bob asked the child's name. With moist eyes, the father replied, "His name was Baby Mohammed, but today we have changed his name to Baby Jesus."

With a look of surprise, Bob asked why.

"Because," the native farmer replied, "we asked Allah to help our baby, and no help came. But we came to Jesus' people, and through them our prayer was answered. So we are dedicating our child to Jesus."

GOD DESERVES OUR LOVE

On the basis of our God's mercies, Paul in Romans 12:1 asks us "to present our bodies a living sacrifice" to God. You may ask, "What is a living sacrifice? If I knew what that meant, I might do it."

In the Old Testament, a dead sacrifice such as a lamb or bull was to be totally consumed by fire. In the New Testament, by contrast, we are to be totally *alive* unto God and dedicated to His service. To be a living sacrifice means making every member of our body—eyes, hands, feet, mouth, heart, ears, brain, *everything*—totally available to Him twenty-four hours each day.

In his paraphrase of Romans 12:1 in the *Living Bible*, Kenneth Taylor says this about the living sacrifice we should make to God: "When you think of what He has done for you, is this too much to ask?" Such a sacrifice on our part is certainly reasonable in view of what God has done for me. Jesus Christ died in my place on the cross—He gave His life for me. He rose from the grave and ascended bodily into heaven where He is now seated at the Father's right hand, interceding for me.

Paul describes this living sacrifice we should make as our "spiritual" service. This word *spiritual* is often misunderstood. It does not mean some vague mood or dreamy attitude. Our bodies are the "temple of the Holy Spirit" (1 Corinthians 6:19). A temple is a very material thing. So are our bodies. Because the occupant of this "temple" is the Holy Spirit, *everything I do* with my material body (not just "official" acts of worship) is a spiritual act. To present my body to God, therefore, is a "spiritual" sacrifice.

How have you responded to the love of Jesus Christ? Have you presented your whole being as a living sacrifice? Is this your way of worship? It is not too late to make this commitment right now. Get alone with God, and give Him your will. Your body will follow.

Total commitment enables the Holy Spirit to control your life consistently. He will furnish guidance in the matter of giving. He will enable you to realize that you are not the owner of your body, your house, your car, even your money. You will find that you do not actually own anything! You and all you have belongs to your Savior; and affliction, poverty, inflation, depression—none of these will affect your relationship to your Savior or how you can give. The risen Savior is your source and the Spirit of God living in you is your wisdom; hence you can give your money with great joy.

Continual renewal of your mind must follow your basic commitment, as Romans 12:2 points out: "Do not be conformed to this world, but be transformed by the renewing of your mind, that you may prove what the will of God is, that which is good and acceptable and perfect" (NASB).

Failure to enter into this essential process of renewal causes our intention to be a living sacrifice to break down. This failure is the reason for the "ups and downs" experienced by many Christians.

How do you renew your mind? The same way you were saved—by faith. God made a promise in the Bible. You needed what God promised, so by faith you accepted the promise and gave Him thanks and obedience. "As ye have therefore received Christ Jesus the Lord, so walk ye in Him" (Colossians 2:6). "Renewal" takes place daily as you claim the promises in God's word by faith.

GIVING IS A GROWING GRACE

God wants us to grow in the "grace" of giving: "But just as you excel in everything—in faith, in speech, in knowledge, in complete earnestness and in love for us—see that you also abound in this grace of giving" (2 Corinthians 8:7, NIV). God not only instructs us to grow in faith, but also to grow in a lifestyle of witnessing and giving to Him. We are to "abound in this grace of giving."

But what if your salary does not increase? God takes care of that, too, because He tells us to grow in the *grace* of giving. This grace comes from God. As you learn to trust God consistently, then God is able to answer your prayers for specific needs on a "gracious" basis. You will not only grow in your love for giving, but you will discover that love always finds a way to give.

A Christian lady once told me of an experience during her life as a seminary student. She was attending seminary on a work scholarship and had no cash income. At Christmas a special offering was being given for missions. God impressed her to make a faith commitment of ten dollars toward that offering. She had no idea how she would be able to write a check for that amount. Soon after she made her faith commitment she received a ten-dollar check from a women's mission group in a church with which she had not had any contact. Through the obedience of both the seminary student

105

and the women's group, a specific need was met on the mission field, and joy accompanied the gift each step of the way.

GIVING IS A TEST OF LOVE

God, through our giving, provides us an opportunity *to prove to ourselves* that we are sincere—that we really love Him. If our giving is a reflection of our love, what does our giving tell us? No one else really knows if we are measuring up to God's desire for our love, but we do.

Regarding their giving, Paul told the Corinthians, "I am not *commanding* you, but I want to test the *sincerity of your love*" (2 Corinthians 8:8, NIV). Our gifts, not just our words, demonstrate the sincerity of our love.

Sincere giving will cause our faith to increase, a process that is part of being "conformed to the image of His Son" (Romans 8:29). As we give, we find joy and peace—blessings from God which nourish our faith in Him. As our faith grows, we grow in victory over sin and worldliness.

Giving then produces more giving as we mature in Christ. This supernatural transformation of our character is no problem, because *God is our source*. He has an ample supply of everything we will ever need. He wants us to give (with the right motives and prompted by His Spirit) so He in turn can meet all our needs.

2 Corinthians 8:9 contains perhaps the greatest example of giving in the whole Bible, and one which is refreshing as we meditate on it: "For ye know the grace

of our Lord Jesus Christ, that, though He was rich, yet for your sakes He became poor, that ye through His poverty might be rich."

The Son of God—who created all, owns all, controls all, and loves all—gave up His heavenly riches and became *poor* for our sakes, so that we might be rich! If you want an example of giving, meditate on our Lord—the giving Christ!

Through His death for us on the cross, Christ accomplished our redemption. He now enables us through faith in His word to have union and communion with the God of the universe. He also empowers us to give, even beyond our means: "With God all things are possible" (Matthew 19:26).

THE PRINCIPLE OF MULTIPLICATION
God's principle of getting His work done is to take what we have and multiply it supernaturally. We see this principle operating in Scripture not only in the matter of money, but in the process of producing disciples. There is a close connection between giving and discipleship, because the essence of a disciple is that he be like Christ; and Christ gave everything—even his life—for ungrateful sinners who did not deserve it. A giving lifestyle is at the heart of being a disciple.

We might state the principle of multiplication this way: When we give what we have to God, he not only multiplies the gift supernaturally, but also uses our example of giving to multiply disciples.

107

Lorne Sanny, president of The Navigators, in his message entitled "What Is That in Your Hand?" points out that when Jesus' disciples took *what they had*, even though it was pitifully small, and *gave it to Jesus*, he multipled a few loaves and fishes so that they became more than enough to feed five thousand people (Matthew 14:15-21).

He notes also that in the Old Testament the dead piece of wood in Aaron's hand (it was all he had) not only became a live branch when blessed by God, but also became an instrument of supernatural power to accomplish God's purpose.

In the same manner, the jawbone of an ass became, under the influence of the Holy Spirit, a weapon in Samson's hand powerful enough to destroy three thousand armed enemies of God.

The principle here is that God can take whatever we give to him, *if it is all that we have*, no matter how insignificant it may be, and multiply our gift so that it becomes more than sufficient for his work.

If you want to get excited about God's promises to multiply our gifts to him, read the *Living Bible* paraphrase of Paul's words in 2 Corinthians 9:10-15—

> For God, who gives seed to the farmer to plant, and later on, good crops to harvest and eat, will give you more and more seed to plant and will make it grow so that you can *give away more and more fruit* from your harvest.

Yes, God will give you much so that you can give away much, and when we take your gifts to those who need them they will break out into thanksgiving and praise to God for your help. So, two good things happen as a result of your gifts—those in need are helped, and they overflow with thanks to God. Those you help will be glad not only because of your generous gifts to themselves and to others, but they will praise God for this proof that your deeds are as good as your doctrine. And they will pray for you with deep fervor and feeling because of the wonderful grace of God shown through you.

The more we adhere to God's principles of giving, the more He will pour out His blessings. God is just waiting to exercise His power through those who will go "all out" for Him as they learn and put into practice His principles for giving.

Whatever else a disciple does, he *gives*. Giving will help fulfill our Great Commission from Jesus Christ to win and train people throughout the earth to become disciples. In fact, without the kind of giving that the Scripture instructs us to do, the carrying out of the Great Commission will fail—not from lack of funds, *but from the lack of godly lives*!

But as Christ's disciples today continue to teach new Christians how to give in a loving way, the new ones too will win and train others to give. If we possess the quality of love expressed by giving, our Christianity will be fruitful and *multiply*. It all starts with giving—God's giving first, then ours.

<u>EVERY GOOD WORK</u>
Many Christians tell me they cannot give to every need that comes along. But let's take a look at one of God's promises: "And God is able to make all grace abound toward you; that ye, always having all sufficiency in all things, may abound to every good work" (2 Corinthians 9:8). God Himself is able to make His grace—His unlimited, unmerited favor—supply everything you need to give joyfully for every good work. When God lays it on your heart to support good works, He will provide enough money to complete the job.

Chapter TEN

GLORIOUS GIVING

GIVE CHEERFULLY

God's principle in giving to us or withholding from us is this: If we sow meagerly, we reap meagerly; if we sow generously, we reap generously. As Paul wrote in 2 Corinthians 9:6-7, "He who sows sparingly will also reap sparingly, and he who sows bountifully will also reap bountifully. So let each one give as he purposes in his heart, not grudgingly or of necessity; for God loves a cheerful giver" (*The New King James Bible*).

God uses the farmer to teach us. If we give little—like the farmer who sows few seeds—we get little in return. If we give much—like the farmer who sows many seeds—we get much more in return.

We must make our own decision, under God's direction, about how much we are to give. We are not to be pushed or forced, but with a *willing heart* we should permit Him to set the amount. The Holy Spirit, whose job it is to instruct, train, and lead us in our decisions, will enlighten our minds. Then our gift will be eagerly given—so that we can hardly wait to sign the check.

Do you give with that kind of eagerness and joy? You should, for God loves a *cheerful* giver, one who purposes in his heart to give to Him, then does it gladly.

GIVE WHOLEHEARTEDLY

Armies have never won battles with halfhearted fighting men. The same is true in the spiritual realm. We give business, sports, travel, education, and sex our wholehearted attention, but many of us are satisfied with just "getting by" in our Christian lives. Yet God has given us this commandment: "Thou shalt love the Lord thy God with all thy heart, and with all thy soul, and with all thy mind, and with all thy strength" (Mark 12:30). Furthermore, God has promised, "You will seek Me and find Me when you seek Me with all your heart" (Jeremiah 29:13, NIV). This is true in our giving as in all areas of life.

GIVE FOR GOD'S GLORY

Years ago I came to the conclusion that the word *glory* seemed to stand for an important doctrine in the Bible, though it was sometimes hard to understand.

The word has many different meanings, but there is

generally one idea which recurs whenever God's glory is discussed: Where God's glory is, there is *the presence of the Lord.* For example, Moses in Exodus 33 asked the Lord to show him His glory. In the same context God said, "My *presence* shall go with thee" (Exodus 33:14). Almost everywhere the term *glory* is used, the *presence* of the Lord is there too.

I am convinced that when we "glorify" God by giving we are actually acknowledging His presence in the act itself. This is one reason why we should not give for the praise of men.

AN ILLUSTRATION OF GIVING

Jesus showed in the parable of the Good Samaritan (Luke 10:25-37) how the Christian will demonstrate his love to Christ through giving. After describing the merciless robbery and assault of a traveler on the road from Jerusalem to Jericho, Jesus portrayed the calloused indifference to his suffering of the religious leaders of that day, who passed by the victim without helping him. But a Samaritan who came by "had compassion on him, and went to him, and bound up his wounds, pouring in oil and wine, and set him on his own beast, and brought him to an inn, and took care of him." He also promised the innkeeper whatever payment necessary to care for the traveler.

What does this story mean for us? Bob Foster in his newsletter, *The Challenge,* applies the parable to our lives today in this way:

A sensitized "Samaritan" conscience costs time, energy, money, reputation, and probably a missed business deal.

The Good Samaritan got his hands dirty in a cause not his own. But it was his own. He made it his cause for he was his neighbor. His involvement conclusively proved that he was touchable, approachable, and lovable. He personalized his faith. He put feet, heart, hands, and pocketbook on his doctrine. Rather than being preoccupied with the temporal, he majored on the monumental!

In stopping and stooping, the Samaritan was not taking time out from his life; he was living his life.

Jesus wants us to learn from this parable that love—for God and for our neighbor—is the fulfillment of the whole law. Giving is the expression of that love. The Good Samaritan shows us how to give. Let's learn the lesson well.

SUMMARY HIGHLIGHTS
The following principles summarize some of the main points we have examined in the Bible's teaching on giving:

• God owns everything. We do not have any absolute rights to ownership of anything, but we hold possessions "in trust" for God (Psalm 24:1).

• After giving God his rightful part—a tithe from our "first fruits"—we are to give in proportion to how God has blessed us, no matter what our income is. This refers to spiritual as well as material blessings.

• God's giving is tied to his *love*. God is love and the greatest example of giving known to man is His giving His Son, Jesus Christ, to die on the cross for our sins. Because love gives, we as members of God's family must give. Because of the Holy Spirit within us, the love of God is active in our bodies; thus we are to give as God gave.

• Jesus said, "Give, and it shall be given unto you" (Luke 6:38). This is the principle on which God works, and this principle never varies. The opposite is true as well—withhold, and you will not receive.

• The basic principle of all giving is that GOD IS OUR SOURCE. He has in store for us all that we will ever need of everything. He has promised to "supply all your needs according to His riches in glory by Christ Jesus" (Philippians 4:19).

• We are instructed by Scripture to share our wealth with those who teach us God's word (Galatians 6:6). This is the basic principle behind the practice of paying pastors and other full-time Christian workers.

• We must yield or present our bodies to Christ as a living sacrifice (Romans 12:1). This is a total commitment on our part. We give everything back to God, who created us and gave us these gifts in the first place. This giving ourselves to God furnishes us with the power and the desire to give His money for His work.

• We are to grow in grace continually—in every-

115

thing. Our faith, witnessing, knowledge of God, love, and giving should grow stronger as we continually experience God's grace. The believer in Jesus Christ is never in a *status quo* situation. He is either advancing or sliding back.

• We give generously to those in need. This giving will be a testimony to others who will glorify God.

• From the early days in the Old Testament, God's people have come to worship bringing gifts. So giving is a form of worship. Do not come to church empty-handed, but bring your gift to God.

HOW TO KNOW YOU ARE GOING TO HEAVEN

The greatest events in the history of the world were the death and resurrection of Jesus Christ.

The crucifixion demonstrates that God in His love to us human beings has given us His most costly gift, the sacrifice of His own Son.

The bodily resurrection of Jesus Christ from the dead three days later proves not only that Jesus is the Messiah of the Old Testament and the God of the universe, but that His death on the cross was sufficient to atone for the sins of the world. The resurrection made the difference between a living Savior or a dead man. And Jesus said, "Because I live, ye shall live also" (John 14:19).

It was necessary in the plan of God for Christ to die and rise from the dead because this was the only way sinful men could enjoy fellowship with a holy God, have a meaningful and abundant life on earth, and go to heaven for eternity after they die.

Either the sinner must die for his sins or an innocent substitute must die in his place. In other words, the penalty must be paid, either by you or by someone else. The death of Jesus Christ, who was a perfect, sinless man yet also the perfect God, was the only sacrifice which could have satisfied God's holy wrath against sin and at the same time demonstrate His divine love for us, His creatures. Only by offering Himself up as our substitute could Christ atone for our sins and take away their penalty and guilt.

Those who believe and receive Jesus Christ, who personally accept by faith God's forgiveness based on Christ's death and resurrection for them, will be saved and receive eternal life. Those who do not accept Christ as Savior will be lost for eternity.

Some key verses in the Bible which explain this truth include Romans 5:8, 1 Corinthians 15:1-6, Hebrews 2:9, and 1 Peter 2:24 and 3:18, all of which I encourage you to read in the *Living Bible*.

These passages reveal God's love which led Him to sacrifice His own Son in order that we might be saved. This is the greatest example of love in human history! God Himself became our sacrifice. The just Man died for unjust men. No ordinary human being could have died in our place. Only the death of Jesus Christ, the God-man, could atone for sins.

We are not only sinners by birth but by practice too. "Yes all have sinned; all fall short of Gods' glorious ideal" (Romans 3:23, *Living Bible*).

If you are asking, "What do I need to do to be saved?" the answer is simple and clear: *You must repent of your sins and receive Christ by faith as your Savior.*

If the Spirit of God has convicted you of your sins and you want to turn from these sins and be saved, and if you are truly sorry for doing wrong and realize your desperate condition before God, the Scriptures say there is a way out for you. Turn in faith to Christ.

You must believe that Jesus Christ died for you on the cross and that He then rose up from the dead. Ask Christ to come into your life, and receive Him as your Savior.

I encourage you to pray this prayer, or one similar to it in your own words:

"Dear Lord Jesus, I know that I am a sinner. I want Your forgiveness. I know that You died on the cross and rose again from the grave for me. I want to turn from my sinful ways. I ask You to come into my life right now and take over, and help me to be obedient to the Scriptures. I want You to have first place in my life—to be Lord of everything I do. Thank You for all of this, and for saving me. Amen."

After you have invited Christ into your life by prayer, studying Bible passages such as those listed

119

below can help you be fully assured of your salvation.

John 10:28   2 Timothy 1:12
Romans 3:38-39   1 John 5:10-13
Romans 10:13   Jude 24-25